ETHNOLOGY OF THE YUCHI INDIANS

ETHNOLOGY OF THE YUCHI INDIANS

FRANK G. SPECK

Introduction to the Bison Books Edition by
JASON BAIRD JACKSON

UNIVERSITY OF NEBRASKA PRESS
LINCOLN AND LONDON

Introduction © 2004 by the Board of Regents of the University of Nebraska
Manufactured in the United States of America

♾

First Nebraska paperback printing: 2004

Library of Congress Cataloging-in-Publication Data
Speck, Frank Gouldsmith, 1881–1950.
Ethnology of the Yuchi Indians / by Frank G. Speck; introduction to the Bison
books edition by Jason Baird Jackson.
p. cm.
Originally published: Philadelphia: University Museum, 1909, in series: Anthropological publications; v. 1, no. 1.
Includes bibliographical references and index.
ISBN 0-8032-9313-5 (pbk.: alk. paper)
1. Yuchi Indians—History.   2. Yuchi Indians—Social life and customs.   I. Title.
E99.Y9S7   2004
305.897′9—dc22
2003027289

This Bison Books edition follows the original in beginning the introduction to the
original edition on arabic page 5; no material has been omitted.

INTRODUCTION

JASON BAIRD JACKSON

First published in 1909, *Ethnology of the Yuchi Indians* is an account of the culture and social life of the Yuchis, a Native American people who reside in the region south and southwest of Tulsa, Oklahoma. This has been their home since the government of the United States forced them to relocate during the 1830s over the aptly named Trail of Tears. Prior to that time, the Yuchis (alternatively "Euchees") lived in town settlements scattered throughout the present-day states of Georgia, Florida, Alabama, Tennessee, and South Carolina.

This book's author, Frank G. Speck (1881–1950), came to know the Yuchis during a series of visits with them that began in 1904—three years before Oklahoma statehood. In the century that has passed since Speck undertook his study, much has changed in Yuchi life. Yet a great many of the customs and traditions that he describes in this work remain central to the community today. When Speck first authored this book, the audience he imagined for it was a small number of scholars working in the still young field of anthropology. Today, the book's readership is much more diverse, and, importantly, it includes Yuchi people who assess its contents in light of their own experience in the culture it describes.

In this context readers of a new edition may raise new questions: What is the book's legacy and what uses does it serve today? Who was Speck and how did he come to make inquiries among the Yuchis? How should the book be evaluated with the passage of time and in light of new knowledge? Drawing upon my own acquaintance with the Yuchi community and my studies of Speck's legacy, I wish to consider briefly some of these questions.

YUCHI ETHNOGRAPHY

Today, as when the anthropologist Speck first visited them, the Yuchis themselves remain the best source of information one can find on Yuchi language, culture, and society. Although members of most Native American communities would make a similar argument for the primacy of their own knowledge, the Yuchi case is special because of the tremendous gap that separates Yuchi knowledge of themselves from that of non-Yuchis. As recently as the 1990s, otherwise responsible scholars mistakenly wrote of the Yuchis as a socially extinct group. Over a long history, leaders of the

United States and the Muscogee (Creek) Nation, who have jointly encompassed and claimed the right to govern the Yuchis, have long described them in a slanderous and ill-informed manner while simultaneously denying their rights of self-governance.[1] More generally, among their non-Native neighbors in eastern Oklahoma today, the Yuchis are almost unknown, largely because they lack the public visibility enjoyed by the state's many federally recognized tribes.

Although a lack of sovereignty is certainly the dominant factor shaping the ways the Yuchis have been misunderstood, the relative paucity of sound scholarly work on the community has also been a hindrance. As an illustration, Harvard University's library, one of the best research collections in the world, holds in total six books dealing with the Yuchis. By contrast, the same library holds seven books on the Creek people published between 2000 and 2002 alone. The total bibliography of works on the Creek and other Native peoples of eastern North America is now quite substantial, at least when measured against the handful of reliable sources available for the Yuchis.[2]

Frank Speck's *Ethnology of the Yuchi Indians* can first be appreciated in this context. Published in 1909 and based on firsthand research undertaken in 1904, 1905, and 1908, it was the first substantive study documenting the culture and social life of the Yuchi people. It remains both the base from which the limited scholarly work that followed it has proceeded and a record, however partial, of Yuchi life at the turn of the twentieth century— a record that Yuchi people continue to use to assess continuities and changes in their own community life. Comparatively, it stands as the only basic ethnography of the Yuchis. Having been published in a limited edition as the inaugural volume in a museum monograph series, the book has long been expensive and hard to come by. This reprinting makes it readily available for the first time.[3]

FRANK SPECK IN YUCHI COUNTRY

Speck came to what was still known as Indian Territory in 1904.[4] Then a twenty-two-year-old graduate student in the new field of anthropology, he had been sent west from New York's Columbia University by his major professor, Franz Boas. Boas's goal for Speck was to document the Yuchi language while recording cultural information and gathering objects of traditional material culture for the American Museum of Natural History. According to the plan formulated by Boas, the American Museum paid for the objects Speck purchased and his travel expenses. To support his actual fieldwork, Boas obtained additional funds from the Bureau of American Ethnology, the anthropological research agency then associated with the

Smithsonian Institution. The primary purpose of this funding was to support Speck's linguistic study of the Yuchi language. Most American Indian languages were then little known and thus deserving of the careful study Boas advocated. The Yuchi language was, and remains, especially interesting because it is a genetic isolate with no demonstrated relationship to other known languages. It was thus of great scholarly interest not only on linguistic grounds but in terms of what its unique status revealed about the cultural history of American Indian peoples in eastern North America.[5]

In late June 1904, Speck arrived in the town of Bristow, the municipality closest to the Yuchi settlement of Sand Creek. Arriving by train, he resided at the Hotel Laurel and traveled during the day by horseback to visit Yuchi as well as Creek consultants. When I first visited Sand Creek's town square in 1995, I traveled in an air-conditioned car over modern roads and bridges; but ninety-one years earlier Speck faced severe practical challenges. Unpublished letters sent from Bristow along with his published writings paint a picture of Indian Territory as an uncomfortable and occasionally dangerous place, a view confirmed by Yuchi oral history. Roads were mere dirt tracks. Rains made rivers and streams impassable. Outlaws from neighboring states sought refuge from the law by hiding in what remained, for a few more years, Indian Territory. Food and other supplies were difficult to obtain, and epidemic diseases were a constant plague. Native people suffered under these conditions while facing the tremendous disruption of having their national governments dissolved and their collective lands broken up and allotted by a government whose promises were never fully realized. This was the world in which Speck sought to make friendly acquaintance with the Yuchis and their neighbors. To make matters worse for him personally, the Smithsonian Institution was plagued by bureaucratic procedures that on several occasions left Speck without the funds to support himself.

Imperfect and incomplete, as all such works must be, this book is nonetheless a record of the remarkable things Speck learned during his visits to the Yuchis. Almost every facet of Yuchi life, from everyday activities to religious beliefs, is treated in this volume. Although the book lacks coverage of the economic and political situation the Yuchis found themselves in at the turn of the century, Speck does treat these matters in some of his popular essays, thereby augmenting the picture of "traditional" Yuchi culture that he makes the focus of this work.[6]

The highlight of Speck's two summer visits was his attendance at Sand Creek town's Green Corn Ceremony.[7] Before his time among the Yuchis, Speck had experienced Woodland Indian culture firsthand in the Northeast, having been partially raised by a Mohegan woman and having learned from her the Pequot language she spoke. Yet these formative experiences were among Northeastern Algonquian peoples who no longer practiced a dramatic tribal ceremonial comparable to the Yuchi ceremonies. Although other Europeans had witnessed the Green Corn Ceremonies of Southeastern peoples, Speck was the first trained anthropologist to do so and to record his observations. While he no doubt faced the suspicions of traditional Yuchi people, particularly during his first visit, he approached his goal with great sympathy for Native religion and an appreciation for its complexities and sophistication. Thus he represented a very different perspective from other non-Indians with whom the Yuchis were in contact— lawless rascals or critical Christians. Despite its scientific tone and occasional misperceptions, the book's descriptions ring true to most Yuchi readers because they lack the moralizing tone typical of non-Indian writings on Indian religion. Speck's reverence and respect for Indian religious life remained a constant throughout his life, and the subject was a topic about which he grew more eloquent as his experiences and friendships accumulated.[8]

Speck returned to Indian Territory for additional studies among the Yuchis in the summer of 1905. At the end of his previous visit, he had anticipated that the work would be more productive on a second visit, when the Yuchis would appreciate the seriousness of his commitment to them and his work. His experience in 1905 seems to have justified this belief; his letters suggest that he accomplished a great deal and gained a clearer understanding of topics only touched upon the year before. Despite such success, though, 1905 proved a more difficult year in practical terms. A yellow fever epidemic is a recurring theme in his letters, as is the difficulty of working in the same August temperatures (with highs in the 100s) that Yuchis now combat with air conditioning. At the end of his second visit, he wrote a simple note to the American Museum of Natural History curator Clark Wissler, declaring: "Have suffered a slight sun stroke & am on my way home leaving tonight. Will write when better" (August 25, 1905). Speck had made it home to his parent's home in Hackensack, New Jersey, by September 6, but he was still ill according to a letter his mother sent to Wissler updating him on her son's condition and whereabouts. Into November 1905 Speck's letters continue to report the lingering effects of his illness, now characterized as a combination of a nervous condition and fatigue, maladies that he attributed to the climate and diet he experienced during his summer work.

After drafting the manuscript of his study, he returned to the Yuchis during the winter of 1908 on a final trip for the purpose of rechecking his findings. Less is known about this trip because by this time Speck was on the staff of the University of Pennsylvania, having been appointed to a fellowship connected with its university museum. In contrast to the volume of letters he wrote back to the American Museum in 1904 and 1905, which remain in the museum's archives, I have discovered no correspondence relating to his trip in 1908.

In American universities at the turn of the twentieth century, a doctoral degree was conferred when a dissertation was published. Apparently because of Speck's student appointment at the University of Pennsylvania, Pennsylvania awarded him his doctoral degree rather than Columbia, where he had been trained. The book reprinted here served as his dissertation, as its original cover reflected with the traditional phrase: "Dissertation presented to the faculty of the University of Pennsylvania for the degree of Doctor of Philosophy." Speck would remain at the university for the remainder of his life and career, founding its department of anthropology in 1913 and training some of the most important anthropologists of the twentieth century.

While the original research mandate Boas gave Speck was to focus on Yuchi language, crafts, and culture, Speck manifested enthusiasm for ethnographic research that would become his own professional hallmark. Speck described in early letters a chance meeting with a group of Kansas (alternatively "Kaws") and his successful work recording Creek music in addition to Yuchi songs, which prompted the following caution from Livingston Ferrand of the American Museum: "Please do not let yourself be led away from the main object of your trip, namely, the Uchee. We know considerable about the Creek already, but about the Uchee, practically nothing; I know from experience the danger there is in dispersing one's attention when in the field" (July 26, 1904). Despite this advice, Speck undertook incidental research among the Chickasaws and Osages. Even more important were the extensive investigations he pursued with Chief Lasley Cloud and other members of the Creek town of Tuskegee, members of which were then participating in the dances and ceremonies of Sand Creek, having abandoned their own ceremonial shortly before Speck's visit. His Creek studies were published in two monographs companion to this one (*The Creek Indians of Taskigi Town* and *Ceremonial Songs of the Creek and Yuchi Indians*) and a series of more specialized scholarly articles. Among the most interesting but least-known products of Speck's visits to Indian Territory is the series of short articles he authored for the popular magazine *The Southern Workman*, published by Hampton Norman and Agricultural Institute. In these Speck describes the chaotic and dangerous nature of life in Indian Territory and highlights the pernicious effects of lawless white grafters, the cultural loss and social instability caused by Christian missionization, and the harm caused by growing racism manifest in such phenomena as racial exclusion towns.[9]

Retrospect

There are many omissions, misunderstandings, and errors waiting to be found in Speck's account. Some are obvious, while others will never be recovered. As a historical document, we are limited in the questions that we may ask of the text. The oldest Yuchis living today had not yet been born during Speck's visit, yet many of the elders prominent in the 1990s knew well the men and women Speck had the good fortune to meet ninety years earlier. These elders—my own teachers—provide me with a living link to the culture that Speck sought to understand and that I continue to seek to understand. Reading Speck's book against their teachings and my own experiences among the Yuchis, I would note several points of potential interest.

The most glaring omission in the book is Speck's failure to note the existence of the fourth major Yuchi settlement among his discussions of Big Pond, Sand Creek, and Polecat towns on page 9. This eastern-most community, known alternatively as Duck Creek or Snake Creek, was located near these two watercourses in the vicinity of present-day Bixby, Oklahoma. Two earlier visitors among the Yuchis, Albert Gatschet and W. O. Tuggle, left records testifying to the existence of Duck Creek in the years before Speck's visit, and my own work has focused on its history and community life in years since his work.[10] Counter to modern geographic expectations, Speck actually entered Yuchi country from the west rather than from the east. He did travel westward by train from his home in New Jersey, but his connections took him first to Paul's Valley in the Chickasaw Nation (sixty miles south of Oklahoma City) and then northeastward to Bristow. Having established himself on the western edge of the Yuchi settlement area, he never saw (during this period) large portions of Yuchi territory.

While reflecting core interests that Speck maintained throughout his long career, *Ethnology of the Yuchi Indians* does not equal the literary style of his later works. It is an able assembly of the facts as best he could establish them; it was difficult work and he was a talented researcher, but one who was still a beginner working in uncharted territory. Demonstrating the value of comparative research, each of Speck's books built upon the lessons and findings of those that preceded it. In later field research among other Native communities in eastern North America, Speck would draw upon his earlier experiences to ask more nuanced questions and to explore topics that he did not yet fully understand while among the Yuchis. Readers of his mature works, such as *The Celestial Bear Comes Down to Earth* and *Midwinter Rites of the Cayuga Long House*, will appreciate a more interesting and artful prose style, but they will also understand the contours of an intellectual journey that began in earnest during his visits to the Yuchis.[11]

For Yuchi readers, a significant disappointment with the *Ethnology of the Yuchi Indians* is that it synthesizes material learned from various Yuchis without specifying who provided Speck with particular information. Elders of today knew the consultants Speck credits in the introduction to the book, but they are disappointed that there is no means of reconstructing the provenance of the information they shared with him. Unfortunately, Speck's papers shed little light on such questions. By way of contrast, in his mature works Speck not only provided detailed biographical information about his consultants but also shared authorial credit with the traditionalists and community scholars with whom he collaborated most intensively.

Speck visited the Yuchis twice during the period surrounding the annual Green Corn Ceremony and once during the winter. These visits provided him an opportunity to experience two very different phases of the yearly round, but he did not experience this annual cycle in its entirety. This was unfortunate because it led to some omissions recognizable with hindsight and also left certain questions unanswered and perhaps unanswerable. Indian football provides an example of a topic capable of being recontextualized, while the nature of fall ceremonialism illustrates a subject about which Speck might have offered otherwise unavailable information.

On page 89 Speck briefly describes the Yuchi football game and illustrates a football that he collected for the American Museum of Natural History. Although Speck describes it briefly and in secular terms, the Yuchi football game is an important ceremonial-ground ritual, one that opens the ritual cycle each spring. Speck was not among the Yuchis during the season in which this game is played, and thus he seemingly did not have the opportunity to learn the full significance of the game. When he encountered ritual football among the Cayuga at the end of his career, he did not recognize that the Yuchis shared this basic Woodland ceremony.[12] This omission is recognizable because manuscript and comparative sources exist, and the game remains central to Yuchi life today. By contrast, Yuchi elders today recall hearing about Yuchi ceremonial gatherings that once took place in the fall, but they did not take part in these themselves and cannot describe them in any detail. Thus, one wonders what Speck might have learned and documented here had he had the luxury of living among the Yuchis for a full year.

Close study of Speck's descriptions of music, dance, and plant medicine here and in his *Ceremonial Songs of the Creek and Yuchi Indians* suggest that these are topics about which his notes became confused. There are discrepancies between the two works in the descriptions he offers, and some of the songs Speck recorded on wax cylinder (transcribed in *Ceremo-*

nial Songs of the Creek and Yuchi Indians by Jacob Sapir) are recognizable by Yuchis today but under different names and with choreographies different from those given by Speck. Such puzzles suggest that Speck's book deserves close reexamination on the basis of new knowledge. A new printing can only assist in such work.

YUCHI COUNTRY SINCE 1908

Changes in a culture are always easier to notice than continuities. In 1908 few Yuchis spoke English as a second language while today few speak Yuchi as a first language. This is a significant change, but look more closely at this Native people's community life and one will see that, despite tremendous forces pressuring the Yuchis to abandon their heritage, they are passionate about retaining their most important traditions. With meager resources, they have invested countless hours documenting, teaching, and learning their language so that this unique expression of Yuchi identity remains a part of their national life. At the time of creation, a set of collective ceremonies was bestowed upon the Yuchis along with the obligation to perform them each year. While this obligation was a challenge for the Yuchi leaders of 1905, as it is for the Yuchi ceremonial ground chiefs today, they and their townspeople continue to meet it. During the second half of the twentieth century, Yuchi ceremonialism became stronger as the community recovered from the disruptions wrought by allotment, World War II, and their full integration into the cash economy. Today the ceremonials ordained by the Creator and described in this book remain a vital part of Yuchi communal life.

Those parts of Yuchi culture and social life that have changed most dramatically are everyday economic and political realities. Like other Americans, the Yuchis experienced social forces in the twentieth century that pushed them from subsistence farming to wage labor in a global market place. Simultaneously, they moved through three stages, each different but linked by the common reality of tribal political disenfranchisement: When Speck first visited, the Yuchis were politically encompassed within the old Creek Nation. Soon after, the Creek Nation was dissolved, and the United States dealt directly with its former citizen as individuals through the Bureau of Indian Affairs. With the devolution of powers and the restoration of tribal governments that took place in the late twentieth century, the Yuchis today are once again subsumed within the Creek Nation. In 1904 Yuchis and their Native neighbors dominated the landscape, at least outside such commercial centers as Tulsa and Bristow. Today Native people reside in a sea of non-Natives, and few families retain lands allotted to their ancestors before statehood. Yet despite such dramatic material and political changes, the core Yuchi values and beliefs Speck encountered remain central to Yuchi life.

Since the time of Speck's visits, the Yuchis have added to this heritage. As Speck predicted, some Yuchi people adopted the Native American Church and its sacramental use of the peyote cactus. Unlike members of the Native American Church in some other tribes, these Yuchis did not abandon the practice of their traditional tribal religion but attended and hosted church services at times when the ceremonial grounds were inactive. In this pattern they followed the lead of their longtime friends the Shawnees as well as their neighbors the Sac and Fox.

In the twentieth century the Yuchi also firmly established two Methodist congregations, one near Sapulpa and the other in Bristow. Unlike the Native American Church members, many (but not all) Methodists stopped participating in stomp dances and town ceremonies. During the early and middle twentieth century, preachers often spoke against these traditions. At the same time ceremonial-ground leaders faced challenges controlling disruptions, such as fighting and drinking, which marred the ceremonies and discouraged participation. By the 1960s strict rules governing participation in ceremonies had resolved these problems. Leaders of the Indian United Methodist Church no longer forcefully condemn ceremonial life, and a greater number of people move back and forth between these two central spheres of Yuchi life.

During the late twentieth century, a growing number of Yuchis drifted away from these distinctly Yuchi religious institutions and participated in non-Indian Christian congregations. Others became involved in broader Indian (as opposed to Yuchi) activities, such as the powwow and gourd dance. Reflecting crosscurrents common in American life, some Yuchis concurrently intensified their commitments to distinctly Yuchi activities and institutions, fuelling the establishment and growth of language classes and camps, genealogy workshops, and a tribal photographic archive as well as a stronger pan-Yuchi tribal organization that continues to seek federal acknowledgement of the tribe as a political entity separate from the Muscogee (Creek) Nation. Thus the late twentieth century offered paradoxes. As the threat of assimilation into the dominant society has grown and some Yuchis have turned their back on tribal life, the community has responded by intensifying its commitments to preserving Yuchi society and its heritage. In doing so, it has strengthened itself and also engaged the interest of numerous tribal members who have grown up with little direct contact with fellow Yuchis.

In these contexts a new printing of Speck's work finds its audience. Yuchi readers need not rely on poor photocopies obtained third hand; and scholars, politicians, and general readers, who have often mistakenly be-

lieved the Yuchis to have disappeared in the midst of their Creek conge-
ners, now have easy access to a basic source that testifies to the Yuchis'
existence as a people possessing a rich and distinctive heritage. While
Speck's accomplishments as a student are worthy of note, the more important story remains the Yuchi people who were his subjects. In this volume
readers encounter the Yuchis of 1904, a remarkable people who maintained a unique way of life despite tremendous hardships. This is a story
that continues into the present: the Yuchis of today similarly have kept
faith with their ancestors and have preserved their unique language, culture, and identity into a new century.

NOTES

1. For a scandalous sample of Creek and European American libel against the
Yuchis, see Amos J. Wright, Jr., *Historic Indian Towns in Alabama, 1540–1838*
(Tuscaloosa: University of Alabama Press, 2003), 171.

2. Constituting the basic literature for Yuchi studies are six works: Frank G.
Speck, *Ethnology of the Yuchi Indians* (reprinted here); Frank G. Speck, *Ceremonial
Songs of the Creek and Yuchi Indians* (Philadelphia: University Museum, Univer-
sity of Pennsylvania, 1911); Günter Wagner, *Yuchi Tales* (New York: Publications of
the American Ethnological Society, 1931); Günter Wagner, *Yuchi* (New York: Columbia University Press, 1934); W. L. Ballard, *The Yuchi Green Corn Ceremonial:
Form and Meaning* (Los Angeles: American Indian Studies Center, University of
California, 1978); and Jason Baird Jackson, *Yuchi Ceremonial Ground Life: Performance, Meaning, and Tradition in a Contemporary American Indian Community*
(Lincoln: University of Nebraska Press, 2003). Missing from but essential to most
libraries is a photographic history edited and published by Euchees United Cultural Historical and Educational Efforts, *Euchees Past and Present* (Sapulpa OK:
E.U.C.H.E.E., 1997). Unpublished archaeological site reports, a few graduate student
dissertations and theses, and a small number of popular and scholarly articles
constitute the remainder of the reliable sources on the Yuchis.

3. Speck titled the book *Ethnology of the Yuchi Indians*, but according to modern usage the book would have been more accurately titled "Ethnography of the
Yuchi Indians." When Speck wrote, the use of the terms *ethnology* and *ethnography*
was still in flux among anthropologists. Both terms embody a range of meanings,
but *ethnography* has over the twentieth century come to refer to descriptions of
particular cultures and social groups; *ethnology* generally refers to comparative or
theoretical work with a broader focus.

4. Discussion of Speck's work among the Yuchis is based on study of his letters
sent from Indian Territory (now preserved in the Department of Anthropology,
American Museum of Natural History, New York) together with archival materials
related to Speck found in the Smithsonian Institution's National Anthropological
Archives (Suitland, Maryland) and at the American Philosophical Society (Philadelphia). Biographical sources include Roy Blankenship, ed., *The Life and Times of
Frank G. Speck, 1881–1950* (Philadelphia: Department of Anthropology, University

of Pennsylvania, 1991) and biographical sketches published in the years following Speck's death, including Horace P. Beck, "Frank G. Speck," *Journal of American Folklore* 64(1951): 415–18, and A. Irving Hallowell, "Frank Gouldsmith Speck, 1881–1950," *American Anthropologist* 53(1951): 67–87.

5. On the basis of his fieldwork, Speck completed a preliminary linguistic analysis of the Yuchi language. It is preserved in manuscripts held by the National Anthropological Archives. The reason this material was not published is a matter of conjecture, but study of the materials suggests that Boas and Speck recognized its linguistic inadequacy. In 1928 Boas sent German anthropologist Günter Wagner back to Yuchi country to attempt further linguistic research, the results of which were published as a collection of texts and a grammatical sketch (see note 2). To Speck's credit, the amount of work he accomplished during a few months living among the Creeks and Yuchis in Oklahoma is remarkable. In a letter dated July 21, 1904, to Livingston Ferrand, assistant curator at the American Museum, Speck wrote: "I find it very difficulty to progress further in obtaining texts which I need most, as few Uchees are proficient in English. However, I am making every effort to secure texts and stories which are about all that I now lack." Among the people of Sand Creek and Big Pond towns there were then few English-speaking Yuchis willing to undertake linguistic work. Undocumented and unrelated to any known language, Yuchi would have represented an extreme challenge of linguistic documentation, particularly in the absence of Native bilingual speakers. Boas and his students represented the cutting edge of descriptive linguistics at the turn of the century, but anthropological linguistics was still in its infancy and Speck lacked the natural gift for language possessed by his friend, fellow student and housemate Edward Sapir. For a review of linguistic research on the Yuchi language as well as a modern descriptive account of the language, see Mary S. Linn, *A Grammar of Euchee (Yuchi)* (Ph.D. Dissertation, University of Kansas, 2001).

6. Speck deals with the political and social realities of Indian Territory at the turn of the century in the following, sometimes biting, essays: "Observations in Oklahoma and Indian Territory," *Southern Workman* 36(1907): 23–27; "Negro and White Exclusion Towns in Indian Territory and Oklahoma," *Southern Workman* 36(1907): 430–32; "The Negroes and the Creek Nation," *Southern Workman* 37(1908): 106–10; and "Missions in the Creek Nation," *Southern Workman* 40(1911): 206–8.

7. Held on July 17–19, 1904, and July 21–23, 1905. See Frank G. Speck, "Indian Ceremonies in Oklahoma and Indian Territory," *American Anthropologist* n.s. 8(1906): 192.

8. Speck's engagement with Native religion and its practitioners is illustrated by the manner in which his Iroquois friends sought to cure his illness near the end of his life, through initiation of Speck into the Dew Eagle Society, and, more surprisingly, how they provided their own ethnographic account of the ceremony on Speck's behalf. See Frank G. Speck, "How the Dew Eagle Society of the Allegany Seneca Cured Gahe'hdagowa," *Primitive Man* 22(1949): 39–59.

9. The two other monographs published by Speck on the basis of his work in 1904-5 are "The Creek Indians of Taskigi Town," *Memoirs of the American Anthropological Association* 2(1907): 100–164, and *Ceremonial Songs of the Creek and*

Yuchi Indians (Philadelphia: University Museum, 1911). In addition to the essays cited in notes 6 and 7, Speck's remaining publications based on his Yuchi fieldwork are "Notes on the Ethnology of the Osage Indians," *Transactions of the Free Museum of Science and Art (University Museum), University of Pennsylvania* 2(1907): 159–71; "Notes on Chickasaw Ethnology and Folk-Lore" *Journal of American Folk-Lore* 20(1907): 50–58; "Some Outlines of Aboriginal Culture in the Southeastern States," *American Anthropologist* n.s. 9(1907): 287–95; "Notes on Creek Mythology," *Southern Workman* 38(1909): 9–11; "Mac Henry, The Bad Man: A Creek Indian's Story," *The Red Man* 4(1891): 9–10, 15; "Yuchi," In *Handbook of American Indians*, Bureau of American Ethnology Bulletin 30, part 2, edited by Frederick Webb Hodge (Washington DC: Bureau of American Ethnology, 1910), 1003–7; "European Tales among the Chickasaw," *Journal of American Folklore* 26(1913): 292; and "Eggan's Yuchi Kinship Interpretations," *American Anthropologist* 41(1939): 171–72.

10. W. O. Tuggle, *Shem, Ham and Japheth: The Papers of W. O. Tuggle* (Athens: University of Georgia Press, 1973); Albert S. Gatschet, "Some Mythic Stories of the Yuchi Indians," *American Anthropologist* o.s. 6(1893): 279.

11. *The Celestial Bear Comes Down to Earth: The Bear Sacrifice Ceremony of the Munsee-Mahican in Canada as Related by Nekatcit* (Reading PA: Reading Public Museum and Art Gallery, 1945); *Midwinter Rites of the Cayuga Long House* (Philadelphia: University of Pennsylvania Press, 1949; reprint, Lincoln: University of Nebraska Press, 1995).

12. Jackson, *Yuchi Ceremonial Life*; Speck, *Midwinter Rites of the Cayuga Longhouse*.

CONTENTS.

CONTENTS.

ETHNOLOGY OF THE YUCHI INDIANS.

INTRODUCTION.

In the summers of 1904 and 1905 I spent a total of about four months among the Yuchi Indians of the Creek nation in Oklahoma collecting material for the Bureau of American Ethnology. The investigation was undertaken at the recommendation of Dr. Franz Boas of Columbia University. Funds to cover transportation and the collection of ethnological specimens were furnished by the American Museum of Natural History upon both occasions under Dr. Boas's recommendation. The greater part of the ethnological material offered in this paper was obtained at the same time, and is published with the permission of both the scientific institutions concerned.

Again during the winter of 1908 while holding a Harrison fellowship at the University of Pennsylvania, I was able under special provision of the Provost to make a third visit to the Yuchi for the purpose of completing my observations, and the studies which are embodied in the present work took their final form during this period.

It has been my object simply to give an account of the Yuchi Indians as they exist at the present day and as they presented themselves to me during my several periods of residence among them, purposely avoiding any lengthy discussion of the conditions which I encountered. Much of the description is based directly upon observation; the rest of the matter was obtained from informants who are responsible for its accuracy

Among the latter were *GΛmbesī'ne* (Jim Brown), *Ekīlané* (Louis Long), *Ka‘Ká* (John Wolf), George Clinton, John Big Pond, *Go^{n}lä^{n}tcīné* (Jim Tiger), Henry Long, and *Fago^{g}o^{n}wī'*, all of whom held civil or religious offices in the tribe, and others who from time to time appeared to be well informed upon special topics.

THE YUCHI INDIANS.

Among the indigenous tribes of the southeastern United States, living within a territory roughly defined by the borders of Georgia and South Carolina, was one, exhibiting a type of culture common to the inhabitants of the country bordering on the Gulf of Mexico east of the Mississippi river, whose members called themselves *Tsoyahá*, "Offspring of the Sun," otherwise known as the Yuchi. Constituting an independent linguistic stock (called Uchean in Powell's classification), their earliest associations, in so far as these are revealed by history and tradition, were identified with the banks of the Savannah river where they lived at a very early time in contact with a southern band of Shawnee, and near the seats of the Cherokee, the Catawba, the Santee, and the Yamasi. These tribes, together with the Yuchi, represent five distinct linguistic stocks; a greater diversity of language than is usually found in so restricted an area east of the Mississippi. The Yuchi maintain that they were originally one of the large tribes of the Southeast which, suffering oppression at the hands of encroaching tribes of the Muskogian stock, became much reduced and was finally incorporated, together with the Shawnee, into the loose coalition of southeastern tribes known in colonial history as the Creek confederacy or the Creek Nation. Indeed it is supposed, and is moreover highly probable, that in the course of extended migrations the Creeks pressed for a considerable length of time upon the Yuchi, who, in a fruitless effort to check the advance of the Muskogi confederacy, resisted the pressure as long as they were able, eventually made peace and themselves joined the league.

HISTORICAL SKETCH

The early historical and literary sources of information about the Yuchi are very meagre indeed.　De Soto in his invasion of the Florida wilderness (1540) is believed to have entered Yuchi territory, and it may be granted that an examination of some names mentioned by his chroniclers would appear to give some color to this belief.[1]　Among other examples of the kind a town named Cofitachiqui, variously spelled, where De Soto was hospitably received by the "Queen," is believed without much hesitation by some writers to have been a Yuchi town.　The Yuchi, however, do not recognize the terms *Cofitachiqui, Cutifachiqui*, or any similar forms of the name given by Biedma, Ranjel, or the Gentleman of Elvas.　On the other hand, evidence of De Soto's contact with the Yuchi is not entirely wanting in these narratives, for we are told of a captive who claimed to belong to a people eastward in a land called "*Yupaha*," which in Yuchi means 'in the distant heights,' (*yūba*, 'far high,' *he* 'in,') or 'the high people' (*yūba, ha* collective particle, 'people').　This piece of evidence stands quite by itself, for it is rather hazardous to attempt to identify with the Yuchi any of the other tribal names given by the Spanish explorers. There is a possibility that the French under Ribault and Laudonniere came in contact with the Yuchi, or at least with tribes of similar culture, at the mouth of the St. John's river at Fort Caroline in 1564, but the evidence furnished by a study of names is not any more satisfactory in this case.　The customs of the natives encountered, however, agree with those of the Yuchi, judging from the pictures made by Le Moyne,[2] the artist of the expedition.

About the year 1729 the Yuchi are supposed to have been gathered on the Chattahoochee river under the protection of the Creek confederacy.　Hardly anything more is heard of the tribe until shortly before 1791, when it was visited by William Bartram of Philadelphia, who recorded a few facts about Yuchi town and its houses.[3]　He thought the Indians numbered 1000 or 1500, as they were said to muster 500 gun men.　Later, in 1798–99, we find the Yuchi described by Benj. Hawkins,[4] as constituting one of the chief towns of the Lower Creeks, located on the right bank of the Chattahoochee river, having three villages and 250 gun men.　His other remarks are not of

---

[1] Narratives of De Soto (in Trailmakers' Series), Vols. I and II.

[2] De Bry, Larger Voyage, Part II, Florida (English).

[3] Travels through North and South Carolina and Georgia, etc., Phila., 1791, p. 388.

[4] Sketch of Creek Country, published in Collection, Georgia Historical Society (1848), p. 62.

much ethnological value. During the Creek War (1813–1814), the Yuchi took a prominent part in affairs, and later removed (1836) with the so-called Creek Nation to the lands beyond the Mississippi river where they are now located. They still maintain to a certain degree their cultural unity in spite of contact with aliens for so long a period. In 1900–1901 some of them joined the Crazy Snake band of Creeks who threatened trouble for the Dawes Commission over the allotment of lands in the Creek Nation.

The main published sources of information on the Yuchi are the following: Albert Gallatin collected and published a vocabulary almost useless on account of inadequate orthography.[1] Gatschet gives some ethnologic notes,[2] a brief summary of the language,[3] three Yuchi myths,[4] and also a very general description of the tribe.[5]

Other references to the Yuchi in literature are mostly quotations from the sources mentioned. A short review of the chief characteristics of Yuchi ethnology is to be found in the Handbook of the American Indians.[6] In a general article on southeastern culture,[7] Yuchi material was also used by the writer for comparative purposes.

The Yuchi, in accordance with their belief that they were the original occupants of eastern Georgia and South Carolina, have no migration legend. Their only myth of this class tells how a part of the tribe broke away from the main stock as the result of a dispute at a dance and departed westward, never to be heard of again. This tradition, like many others, is found widely distributed over America in various guises and evidently reflects certain elements common to Indian mythology rather than an actual experience of the tribe relating it. At the same time the Indians have a very firm belief that another band of Yuchi is somewhere in existence, a belief which, while it has nothing to support it except the stories that they tell, should not, perhaps, be altogether ignored.[8]

[1] American Antiquarian, Vol. II (1836), pp. 306 *et seq.*
[2] Ibid. (1879), p. 77.
[3] Science, Apr., 1887, p. 413.
[4] American Anthropologist, Vol. VI (1893), p. 280.
[5] Migration Legend of the Creek Indians (1884), Vol. I, pp. 17–24, Vol. II, passim.
[6] Bulletin 30, Bureau American Ethnology (1907), part 2.
[7] American Anthropologist, N. S., Vol. 9, No. 2 (1907), pp. 287–295.
[8] A chief related the following incident in mentioning this tradition. "I was in Muskogee (Oklahoma). I passed an Indian on the street. We spoke together. He said he was a Yuchi from near the mountains. We could understand each other, but he was not a Yuchi of our country. I don't know where he belonged or where he went. He may have been one of the other band." On another occasion some Yuchi who were attending an Indian show were addressed by a strange Indian in the following words: "Wīgyä' nénAⁿ," 'What are you?' They observed, they say, a slight difference between his speech and theirs, but before they could find out from him where he came from he was called away by someone and they could not find him again. The Yuchi talk a great deal about these occasions, and seem to have hopes of finding the lost people some day.

POPULATION.

At the present day the Yuchi are located in the northwestern part of the Creek nation, where they have been since the removal in 1836. They inhabit the well-watered hills in the section known locally as the Cross Timber, a thinly wooded tract running in a general northerly and southerly direction through central Oklahoma, the last extensive frontier of timber on the southwestern prairies marking the old boundaries of Oklahoma and Indian Territory. There are in this region three so-called settlements of Yuchi, called respectively Polecat, Sand Creek and Big Pond by the whites. All of these settlements are distributed in a region extending from Polecat Creek to the Deep Fork of the Canadian river. When, however, the term settlement is used for such inhabited districts it is a little misleading because, although the Indians are a little more closely grouped in the three neighborhoods mentioned, they are really scattered over the whole of the Cross Timber country, none of which is thickly settled by them. Their plantations, where they engage in agriculture or in cattle raising, are not in close proximity to each other, except where some passable road and the nearness to good water and arable soil combine to attract them. In such cases there may be a dozen families found within the radius of a mile or so. In some parts of their habitat, however, ten or twelve miles of forest and prairie affording good cover for game may be traversed without passing a plantation. Thus, according to their own accounts as well as those of their neighbors the Creeks, the Yuchi were accustomed to live in their old homes in Georgia and Alabama.

It is a very difficult matter at present to estimate the number of the Yuchi on account of their scattered condition. As no separate classification is made for them in the government census they are counted as Creeks. Their numbers, however, can hardly exceed five hundred. They are apparently most numerous in the vicinity of Polecat Creek. The other neighborhoods are somewhat less populous but are regarded as being a little more conservative.

Despite the fact that three settlements are recognized by themselves and their neighbors, the Yuchi constitute only a single town in the eyes of the Creeks. The latter, as is well known, had a national convention in which delegates were received from all the towns and tribes of the confederacy. Accordingly the Yuchi, as one of the confederated town-tribes, had the privilege of sending one representative to the House of Kings and four to the House of Warriors, as they called the two political assemblies of the Creek Nation at Muscogee. This convention met once a year until 1906 and was a modified and modernized survival of the form of assembly held in the old days by the tribes constituting the Muskogian alliance. These bodies met irregularly to consider questions which arose between them, as a loosely united league, and the United States Government or other tribes. If the numerical strength of the tribe recorded by Bartram in 1791 and Hawkins in 1798–99 can be regarded as approximately correct the Yuchi must now be on the decrease. Bartram thought there were 500 gun men, and Hawkins stated, only a few years later, that there were 250 gun men. In any case, granting the existence of inaccuracies in both estimates, it is safe to conclude that the numbers of the Yuchi, like the other surviving tribes of the Southeast, have dwindled slightly in the last hundred years. Numerical comparisons of this sort between past and present are, however, of very little value, as can be seen from the wide discrepancies in the early estimates.

ENVIRONMENT.

NEIGHBORS.

The Yuchi of the present time have nearly forgotten their old associations east of the Mississippi. Their geographical knowledge is practically limited to their immediate surroundings. They are known to the Creeks as *Yū'tci*, plural *YūtcA'lgi*, to the Cherokee as *Yū'tsi*, and to the Chickasaw as *Yū'tci*. An informant stated that they were known to the Comanche as *SakyówA^n*.

To the Yuchi their near neighbors the Creeks are known as *Kū'ba*, 'looking this way' (?), plural *Kū'baha*. The Shawnee they call *Yo$^{n'}$cta*, the Cherokee *Tsala''ki*, and the Choctaw *Tca^ɛ'ta*. Their name for whites in general is *Ka''ka* (*Goyáka*) 'man white,' for negroes *Go'cpi*, 'man black.'

In their bearing towards other tribes it is noticeable that the Yuchi hold them in some contempt. They seldom mix socially with the Creeks, presumably because of their former enmity. A strong feeling of friendship is, however, manifested toward the Shawnee, which is probably a sentiment surviving from early affiliation with the southern branch of this people on the Savannah river.[1] It should be added, however, that the Shawnee who associate with the Yuchi are not part of the large band known as the Absentee Shawnee of Oklahoma. The former are not at all numerous, but live scattered among the Yuchi villages.

With their neighbors on the west, the Sauk and Fox, the Yuchi have developed, since the removal, considerable intimacy. Their contact can be traced in trade, in attendance upon each other's ceremonies, and especially in the Plains practice of "sweating" horses, which will be described later. It is not impossible that some of the items of Yuchi culture, particularly in decorative art, may be found to have been derived from the Sauk and Fox when more is known on both sides.

The following translation from the beginning of a myth, describing the way in which the tribes were distributed over the earth, shows the Yuchi concept regarding the origin of their neighbors: "Now the people had come upon the earth. The Shawnee came from above. The Creeks came from the ground. The Choctaw came from the water. The Yuchi came from the sun."

---

[1] Cf. Linguistic map of North American Indians, Algonkian area near Uchean (Yuchi); Mooney, Myths of the Cherokee, 19th Report, Bureau American Ethnology, p. 494; Siouan Tribes of the East, p. 83; Schoolcraft, North American Indians, Vol. V, p. 262 *et seq.* (1791); Benj. Hawkins, sketch of Creek Country (1798–99), pp. 34, 63.

Like many Indians the Yuchi show in their manner and speech not a little suspicion and some contempt for the whites, whom they believe to be fickle and weak. These qualities are ascribed by the Yuchi to the manner of their origin, for it is explained in a myth that the white men originated from the unstable foam of the sea which is ever blown hither and thither by the changing winds. When first seen they were thought to be sea gulls, but they appeared to the Yuchi again and tried to converse with them. Once more, when a year had passed they appeared again in numerous ships and this time they landed, but left before long. Another time they appeared, bringing boxes which they filled with earth in which they planted some seeds. They told the Indians that their land was fat, *i. e.* fertile, and asked for a portion of it to live upon. With this request the Indians complied, and the white people made a settlement and stayed. One cannot fail to suspect that this bare tradition contains a memory of Ribault's expedition to Carolina and his settlement at the mouth of the St. John's river.

The negroes on their part do not challenge much attention from the Yuchi. The Indians are perhaps more tolerant of what they regard as foolish behavior and frivolity on the part of the black man than on the part of the white man. At one time the Yuchi, like the other tribes of the Southeast, held slaves, but it is said of them that they were easy masters, and when the time came to do so, gave the negroes their freedom with little reluctance. It is true today that many negroes, and some poor whites as well, are eager enough to work for the Indians on their plantations.

It may be said in general that the Yuchi are regarded by their neighbors and compatriots the Creeks with some dislike, tinged, however, with jealousy and a little personal fear. The Creeks are fond of ridiculing the conservatism and peculiarities of the Yuchi, but they take care not to do so openly or to provoke personal disputes with them.[1] It is noticeable that there exists a slight difference in physical appearance between the two peoples. The Yuchi are a little more inclined to be tall and slender than the Creeks and their skin is a trifle lighter in tone. These differences may be due to a mixture of negro blood, for the percentage of persons of mixed blood among the Yuchi, who, however, have received some admixture from both white and black, is smaller apparently than that observed among the Creek, Seminole and Cherokee. So far as the Yuchi are concerned the process of cross-breeding must have begun at an early date because many of those who show intermixture have no direct

---

[1] A Creek Indian of Kawita town, for instance, gave the following belief in regard to the Yuchi and their language: "When the Creator made the ancestors of the Indians he gave them different languages until he had none left. He found that there were still some Indians whom he had not provided for. These were the Yuchi. Having no language for them, he kicked them in the buttocks saying 'BA!' which explains why the Yuchi have such an unintelligible speech."

knowledge of any other than Indian ancestry. Their conservatism in this respect is shown by the fact that notwithstanding the long period of time during which the Yuchi have been in contact with other tribes and races there are very many pure bloods among them at the present day.

Calling themselves "Sun Offspring," the Yuchi believe in reality that they derive their origin from the Sun, who figures in their mythology as an important being of the supernatural world. He appears as their culture hero after the creation of the tribal ancestor from a drop of menstrual blood. The name Yuchi ($Y\bar{u}'tc\bar{\imath}$), however, is commonly known and used by themselves and the whites and has spread among neighboring Indians as the designation of the tribe. It is presumably a demonstrative signifying 'being far away' or 'at a distance' in reference to human beings in a state of settlement, ($y\bar{u}$, 'at a distance,' $tc\bar{\imath}$, 'sitting down').

It is possible, in attempting an explanation of the origin of the name, that the reply "$Y\bar{u}'tc\bar{\imath}$" was given by some Indian of the tribe in answer to a stranger's inquiry, "Where do you come from?" which is a common mode of salutation in the Southeast. The reply may then have been mistaken for a tribal name and retained as such. Similar instances of mistaken analogy have occurred at various times in connection with the Indians of this continent, and as the Yuchi interpreters themselves favor this explanation it has seemed advisable at least to make note of it.

In the almost universal sign language of the Plains the sign for the Yuchi is the right hand raised level with the head with the index finger pointing upward; a demonstration indicating affiliation with the sun.

NATURAL ENVIRONMENT.

The natural surroundings of the Yuchi have not been very different in the various locations which they have occupied east of the Mississippi. Even after the removal of these Indians to their present habitat west of that river, the nature of their environment was not found to be so different as to force them to make much change in their manner of life. That is to say, the keynote of their activity was and still is agriculture supplemented by hunting and fishing. The motives for the accompanying arts of basket making and pottery, together with methods of warfare, hunting, fishing and religious observances, have all likewise remained about the same since the removal. Unlike the Siouan peoples who, when they migrated from the Mississippi basin to the Plains, gave up their agricultural life entirely and became hunting nomads, the Yuchi retained their early mode of life amid their new surroundings and transported, with little change, their old activities. In their new home in Oklahoma they found arable soil, plenty of rivers containing edible fish, and extensive forests and savannahs inhabited by birds and mammals like those of Georgia and Alabama.   Both regions are rather low and well watered and are characterized by extensive grassy uplands and patches of forest, differing to some extent in regard to flora but containing many species in common.   Chief among these are the pines, the oaks, the hickory, and the bois d'arc, as well as many wild plants and vegetables made use of for food or medicines.   The chief plants used in their religious rituals, Red root (*Salix tristis* (?) and Button Snake root (*Eryngium yuccaefolium*), are distributed over both areas; consequently the Yuchi were not forced to substitute, in the performance of religious ceremonies, other plants for those prescribed by tradition.   One vegetable product, however, the cane, is not as abundant in Oklahoma as it is in the Southeast, and the lack of this plant has occasioned the deterioration in the art of basket making and has even threatened it with total extinction.   Canes for basketry can be secured nowadays only by making long journeys to distant swampy sections and consequently remarkably few cane baskets are seen.

The fauna of the two regions is for the most part alike.   The Indians knew and utilized in both regions the bison, elk, Virginia deer, black bear, wolf, fox, panther, wildcat, beaver, rabbit, squirrel, raccoon, possum, skunk, weasel, and otter.   Common to both regions too are the wild turkey, partridge, quail, wild pigeon, mallard duck, teal and wild goose.   Eagles and herons furnished the feathers appropriate for ceremonial uses in the new home as in the old.   But in leaving the Southeast they left behind the alligator, and encountered the prong-horned antelope and coyote, and they noticed changes in the number and distribution of their former animal acquaintances.   Lastly the streams and rivers of Oklahoma were found to contain the fish which had been familiar and useful in the Southeast, namely catfish, dogfish, suckers, garfish, pickerel, mullets, and several kinds of bass.

The summers of Oklahoma, like those of Georgia and Alabama, are long and hot, but the winters west of the Mississippi are somewhat colder and more severe than in the Southeast.   This change of climate has had its detrimental effect upon the Yuchi, for it seems that their habits of life are not so well adapted to the severer western winters, and most of their present sufferings are due to exposure at this time of the year.   On the whole, however, the Yuchi, men, women and children, are a remarkably strong and healthy set of people.

LANGUAGE.

My original purpose in visiting the Yuchi was to collect linguistic matter, which is now being worked up for special purposes in the interest of the Bureau of Ethnology. Although the detailed results of my linguistic studies are not available for the present paper it will be of advantage to introduce here a general statement regarding some characteristics of the language.

It is quite certain now that Yuchi is spoken in only one dialect, although there is a current opinion that formerly the stock was more numerous than it is at present and that the language was spoken in two dialects. These dialects are stated according to tradition to have been mutually intelligible when spoken slowly. The language is characterized as regards processes by the use of postpositional and prepositional particles to show local modification of the noun, and by the use of auxiliaries to show adverbial and modal qualification of the verb. Position also plays some part in the expression of adverbial modification, verbal subordination, and sentence syntax. Inflection is not a characteristic of Yuchi, and reduplication is only used to denote the idea of distribution in time and space. The parts of speech seem to be nouns, verbs, adverbs, pronouns and particles. There are no syntactical cases, as in the neighboring Muskogian. The position of words indicates their syntactical relationship. Neither do there appear to be case affixes; the whole range of such ideas, locatives, instrumental, simulative, ablative, demonstratives and others being expressed by particles. In this class are also the temporal, modal and other particles used with verbs. There are a number of monosyllabic local and adverbial particles which have very general meanings. These syllables may enter into combination with each other and form thereby new word complexes which may have arbitrary meanings not necessarily derivable from the logical sum total of the thoughts expressed by them. Such compounds may be used as new verbs, new nouns, adverbs or auxiliaries. This psychological trait of Yuchi is, however, not an uncommon one in other American languages. There is apparently no true plural, either in nouns or verbs. The place of the plural is taken by the distributive idea which is expressed by reduplication. Verbs are mostly monosyllabic, but many have developed by combination into polysyllabic forms impossible to analyze. Nouns are of the same sort. In the noun compound the possessive pronominal elements are quite prominent, and their place is often taken by particles going with the name of the object, and immediately before it, which denote its possessor. These possessive particles, however, do not mark off any particular categories. As in other American languages, many verb and noun stems are difficult to distinguish apart. The difficulty of distinguishing between verbs and nouns is further increased by the homology between the possessive pronominal and the active subject pronominal forms. As regards personal pronouns, we find only two categories, both of which are closely related. Whether active or neutral, transitive or intransitive, the subjective pronominal forms are the same. In this paradigm are also included the possessive pronominal forms. The other category is the objective which in all but the first and second persons is a development of the subjective or of the absolute, independent forms. All of the pronominal forms are independent words capable of standing by themselves. In the pronominal persons we have first, second, third masculine, third feminine (both of which refer more particularly to Yuchi Indians), and a third indefinite form which includes whites, negroes, other Indians, animals and indefinite objects in general. Besides these forms, which are all singular, there is a first person plural and a second person plural. No difference is recognized in the pronouns between the third person singular and plural.

To conclude this brief sketch, it may be said that the whole sentence, hinging upon the verb, which comes last in position, is built up with various locative, adverbial, and pronominal particles which have fairly definite places in the sentence but which are not inseparably affixed to the words they refer to. Thus the sentence may be built up more and more, expressing details by simply stringing on particles or particle compounds with arbitrary meanings before one another, the verb, immediately preceded by its pronouns and these by its adverbs, coming last.

The subject of phonetics has been left until the last in order to make a somewhat special mention of the sounds and characters to be used in recording terms hereafter. The language, generally speaking, is acoustically soft and flowing and abounds in arrested sounds and nasalized vowels. The present-day Yuchi assert that they speak more rapidly than the old-time people, and, they add, the purer forms of the expressions are often mutilated in consequence. Another notice in connection with phonetics should be made here in outline at least. It is the constant tendency to combine phonetically pronouns with words, and words with other words, when certain vowels and semivowels come together at the beginning and end of words. This phonetic coalescence has a tendency to obscure some particles and to knit parts of the sentence into a closer unity, giving the whole something of the appearance of incorporation where it really does not exist. The following is an explanation of some of the sounds encountered in the recording of terms, and the characters which represent them.

In the stops we have the glottal catch represented by ${}^{\varepsilon}$. The palatal surd k and sonant g are both similar to the English sounds. The alveolar dentals *t* and *d* and the labials *p* and *b* are found, both pairs being rather difficult to determine as to their surd and sonant quality. In the spirants we have the palatal *c* like English sh, and the surd *tc*, a single sound, like ch as in English church, with the corresponding sonant *dj*. The alveolars are *s*, *ts*, and *dz*, similar to the English sounds. The labial dental surd *f* occurs, but there is no corresponding sonant. All of the surds given so far occur also followed by a catch and are represented in such cases as follows, t^ε, p^ε, tc^ε, s^ε, f^ε, etc. The nasal *n* occurs, but independent *m* is wanting. The lateral spirant surd sound made by pressing the tip of the tongue against the upper alveolar ridge and forcing the breath out over both sides of the tongue, is represented by *ł*. A common *l* like that in English is also found. The semivowels are *h*, *y*, *w;* and the bilabial aspirate of the last *hw*, also occurs.

The vowels are *a*, *e*, *i*, *o*, *u*, with their continental values. They are short when not marked; long with the mark over them as *ā*, *ē*, *ī*, *ō*, *ū*. Other long vowels are *â* like a in English fall, and *ä* like a in English fan. Besides these there is an obscure vowel represented here by ʌ which is similar to u in English but. Nasalized vowels, which are very frequent, are written a^n, $ä^n$, $â^n$, etc. Breathed vowels are *a'*, ʌ', etc. The diphthong *ai* occurs rarely. Stress and prolongation are indicated by !. Accent is marked by '.

MATERIAL CULTURE.

AGRICULTURE.

Although the Yuchi of today are cultivators of the soil, as they were in former times, the manner and method of agriculture has undergone many radical changes since the first contact with Europeans. The modification of this branch of their culture has been so thorough that we can only construct, from survivals and tradition, an idea of its former state.

The villages were surrounded by fertile spaces, cleared of timber and other vegetation by burning in dry springtime.   These spaces were converted into garden patches where vegetables were sown and tended as they grew up, by a daily but irregularly-timed cultivation.

It is not now remembered whether particular parts of the arable ground were the personal property of the individuals or clans. Hawkins states, however, that both men and women labored together; the Yuchi differing in this respect from the Creeks. The old people and children found daily employment in acting as guardians over the growing crops, in driving away crows, blackbirds and other troublesome creatures.

In general, the land of the tribe belonged to whosoever occupied or utilized it.   The boundaries of fields, plantations and real estate holdings, where encroachment was likely to occur, were marked by upright corner stones with distinguishing signs on them to indicate the claim.   A man would simply adopt some optional design or figure as his brand and make this his property mark. Trees were also blazed to mark off property limits. In blazing, a piece of bark about as large as the hand was sliced off about five feet from the ground, leaving the white wood exposed. Sometimes the space was marked with pigment.   The above devices are still in common use throughout the Creek Nation.

The most important native vegetables were flint corn, *tsot$^\varepsilon$o'*, beans, *tsodi'*, sweet potatoes, *tosä$^{n'}$*, melons, *tcä^n*, pumpkins and squashes. These are believed to have been given the Yuchi by the supernatural being, Sun.   Tobacco, *i'tci̅*, was grown by each family near the house.   This was believed to have originated from drops of semen.   The plant was named by a boy, in mythical times, and distributed among the people for their use.   When tobacco was smoked sumach leaves were added to it.   Gourds were also raised, to be used as household receptacles.

When the crops of corn and other vegetables were taken in they were stored away in outhouses and cribs, *dadá*, raised on posts, to be used when wanted.

Before the harvest could be devoted to general use, however, it was thought necessary to perform certain ceremonies of personal purification and propitiation in behalf of the supernatural beings who gave the crops and who brought them to maturity.   Taking into account the number and importance of such rites together with the amount of daily time and labor that was devoted to the cultivation of the crops, we are led into the general classification of the Yuchi as an agricultural type of people.

HUNTING.

Hunting was pursued by the men either singly or in bands.   While the attendance upon the crops kept them at home much of the time, there were seasons of comparative idleness during which parties set off on the hunt. The flesh of nearly all the mammals and birds of their habitat was eaten by the Yuchi with the exception of such as were sacred for ceremonial purposes or were protected by some taboo.   The chief game animals hunted by them for their flesh were the deer, *wēᵋyᴀⁿ'*, bison, *wedīngá*, bear, *sagᵋē'*, raccoon, *djatyᴀⁿ'*, opossum, *wᴀtsagowᴀⁿ'*, rabbit, *cádjwané*, squirrel, *cayá;* while those whose skins were chiefly sought after were the panther, *wetcᵋᴀⁿ'*, wildcat, *pocī'*, fox, *cadᵋané*, wolf, *daɫá*, otter, *cuɫané*, beaver, *cagäⁿ'*, and skunk, *yūsᵋᴀⁿ'*.   The flesh of these was also eaten at times.   Wild turkeys, *wetcᵋä'*, quail, *späⁿsī'*, partridge, ducks, geese and other birds were continually hunted for food.

The game animals were believed to be very cunning and wise in knowing how to avoid being captured.   So in order to blind their senses, and to overcome their guardian spirits, the magic power of certain song burdens was employed by hunters.   Shamans held these formulas in their possession and could be induced to accompany the hunting party to the field to aid in the bewitching of the quarry.   Shamans might also teach the formula to some one for the same purpose, upon the payment of some price or upon being promised a share in the spoils.

One of these songs used for charming the deer is,

ya ha gi do gi do da ni ho ya ha gi

do gi do gi do* da ni ho. haiⁿ yä.
(*Spoken.*)

*The syllables *gi do* are sometimes given three times, sometimes four, with no seeming regularity.

Not only had the hunter himself to be careful to keep the game animals and supernatural protectors well disposed toward him by observing all the taboos, but those connected with him in any way had to be careful too.   This was particularly true in regard to his wife.   Her main care was to remain faithful in her husband's absence, no matter how long he might be away.   Any remissness on her part would cause his guiding spirit to leave him and then his hunt would turn out unsuccessful.

Besides these magic aids the Yuchi made use of more material means to bring down game.   The bow and arrow and blowgun were the chief hunting implements, while a kind of deer call was carried on a string about the neck to call the bucks during the rutting season and the does when they were rearing their fawns.

The bow, *estadē'* (Fig. 1), is a single almost straight stave of bois d'arc

Fig. 1.   Bow.

(*Toxylon pomiferum*) or Osage Orange, about five feet in length.   Sassafras and hickory bows were sometimes made.   No backing of sinew is known to have been used.   The stave is broadest in the middle, where it is about one and one-half inches in width, tapering to one inch at the ends.   The thickness of the stave is about three-quarters of an inch.   The rich dark color of the wood is brought out by greasing.   In section the bow is almost rectangular. The ends are cut out into little knobs of several shapes (Fig. 2) to hold the

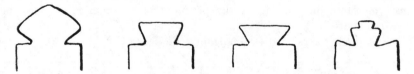

Fig. 2.   Bow Notching.

string.   The bow string is made of deer sinew, $ya^nh\bar{\imath}'$, or strips of rawhide twisted tightly.   Squirrel skins are much in use for bow strings.   The skin is cut around the edge spirally toward the center, thus giving a single long strip. As extra strength is desired, four such strips are twisted together, forming quite a thick cord.   A guard, $go^ns\ddot{a}j\ddot{a}n\acute{e}$, of leather is used by archers to protect the wrist from the bow string when this is released.   The guard is bound on by two thongs attached to holes in the leather (Fig. 3).

Arrows, *la cū'*, for hunting are made of the straight twigs of arrow-wood or of cane stalks of the proper thickness (Fig. 4). In the former case it was only necessary to scrape off the bark and season the twigs. The Yuchi do not seem to have had the idea of the fore-shaft. The point, *lacipá*, which was formerly of stone is nowadays made of iron and is bound by means of sinew into a split in the shaft (Fig. 4). The arrows are feathered preferably with hawk feathers, as the Indians believe the hawk to be swift and sure in

Fig. 3. Wrist Guard.

its flight. Turkey tail feathers are much used also. The split plumes, two in number, are bound to the shaft at both ends with sinew. One side of the feather is shaved clean of ribs up to within an inch of the outer end. The lower or base end of the quill is then lashed on flat.

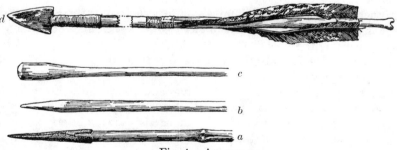

Fig. 4. Arrows.

The outer end is turned down and the turned down length is lashed on. In this way an ingenious twist is given to the feather, which causes the arrow to revolve in its flight, acting on the principle of the rifled bullet (Fig. 4, d). There is some diversity in the length of the arrow shaft and in the size of the arrow head. For killing large game and in warfare the shafts used are almost three feet long with iron triangular arrow heads. But in hunting small game they have simple round sharpened shafts which are seasoned in heat to make them stiff (Fig. 4, b).   The arrows used for shooting fish are somewhat different from the ones described above, as we shall see.   Blunt wooden-headed arrows, so common everywhere, were also used for stunning small animals and birds (Fig. 4, c).

The arrow shaft in all cases is cylindrical, and of the same width throughout.   In some specimens, however, there is a slight widening at the notch to give a better grip.   Several instances were also noticed where there were two notches at right angles to each other.   This feature, according to the native idea, makes it possible for the shooter to send his arrow so that the iron point is either vertical or horizontal.   In the former case the point passes more readily between the ribs of deer, bison and other animals, while in the latter case it is designed to pass between the ribs of man.   The double notching also facilitates adjustment in rapid shooting.   An old arrow, one that has seen use, is thought to shoot better and to be more effective in general than a new one.   In shooting with the bow it is held nearly vertically, the release to the string being given by the index finger, between the third joint of which and the thumb the butt of arrow is grasped.   The release, in general terms, comes nearest to that described by Mason as the tertiary release.[1]

One form of the blowgun, which is obsolete now, was, according to memory, made of a cane stalk with the pith removed.   It was between five and a half and six feet long.   The darts were made of hard wood, the points being charred and sharpened.   A tuft of cotton wrapped about the end of the dart like a wad formed the piston.   This was almost exclusively used for bringing down small animals, squirrels and birds.

Another part of the former hunter's outfit was, frequently, a stuffed deer head which he put over his shoulders or elevated on a stick in front of him when he was approaching the deer.   Thus disguised he could be surer of getting a favorable shot.   The formula given above was sung at intervals during this process of getting nearer.

Dogs, *tsené*, have always been the invariable companions of the hunters, whether alone or in bands, their principal office being to track game and hold it at bay.   The present Indian dogs are mongrels showing intermixture with every imaginable strain, but the wolfish appearance and habits of many of them would suggest that their semi-domestic ancestors were of the wolf breed.

Hunters are usually proficient in calling wild turkeys by several means. One instrument made for this purpose is the hollow secondary wing bone of the turkey, about five inches in length.   The hunter draws in his breath through this tube, making a noise which can best be described as a combination of

---

[1] North American Bows, Arrows and Quivers, O. T. Mason, Smithsonian Reports (1893), p. 636.

smacking, squeaking and sucking. By skillfully operating the calls the birds are lured within range. Sometimes the palm of the hand is employed in making the noise. Another device is to grate a piece of stone on the top of a nail driven fast into a piece of wood. The rasping sound produced in this way will answer quite effectively as a turkey call if manipulated with skill.

The Yuchi do not seem to have used the deer fence so common in many parts of America. They have been known, however, to employ a method of driving game from its shelter to places where hunters were stationed, by means of fire. Grassy prairies were ignited and when the frightened animals fled to water they were secured by the band of hunters who were posted there.

The deer call, *wēᵋyᴀⁿkané*, mentioned before, which is used in calling deer within range, is a rather complex instrument and probably a borrowed one, at least in its present form (Fig. 5). A hollow horn is fitted with a wooden mouthpiece which contains a small brass vibrating tongue. When blown this gives a rather shrill but weak sound which can be modified greatly by blowing softly or violently. A tremulous tone

Fig. 5. Deer Call.

like the cry of a fawn is made by moving the palm of the hand over the opening of the horn. Much individual skill is shown by the hunters in using this instrument.

FISHING.

Quite naturally fishing plays an important part in the life of the Yuchi who have almost always lived near streams furnishing fish in abundance. Catfish, *cū djᵋá*, garfish, pike, *cū cpá*, bass, *cū wadá*, and many other kinds are eagerly sought for by families and sometimes by whole communities at a time, to vary their diet. We find widely distributed among the people of the Southeast a characteristic method of getting fish by utilizing certain vegetable poisons which are thrown into the water. Among the Yuchi the practice is as follows. During the months of July and August many families gather at the banks of some convenient creek for the purpose of securing quantities of fish and, to a certain extent, of intermingling socially for a short time. A large stock of roots of devil's shoestring (*Tephrosia virginiana*) is laid up and tied in bundles beforehand. The event usually occurs at a place where rifts cause shallow water below and above a well-stocked pool. Stakes are driven close together at the rifts to act as barriers to the passage and escape of the fish. Then the bundles of roots (Fig. 6) are thrown in and the people enter the water to stir it up. This has the effect of causing the fish, when the poison has had time to act, to rise to the surface, bellies up, seemingly dead. They are then gathered by both men and women and carried away in baskets to be dried for future use, or consumed in a feast which ends the event. The catch is equally divided among those present.   Upon such an occasion, as soon as the fish appear floating on the surface of the water, the Indians leap, yell and set to dancing in exuberance.   If a stranger comes along at such a time he is taken by the hand and presented with the choicest fish.

As the fish are taken out they may be cleaned and salted for preservation, or roasted and eaten on the spot.   A favorite method of cleaning fish the instant they are caught, is to draw out the intestines with a hook through the anus, without cutting the fish open.   A cottonwood stick shaved of its outer bark is then inserted in the fish from tail to head.   The whole is thickly covered with mud and put in the embers of a fire.   When the mud cracks off the roast is done and ready to eat.   The cottonwood stick gives a much-liked flavor to the flesh.

In the way of a comparison, we find that the Creeks use pounded buckeye or horse chestnuts for the same purpose.   Two men enter the water and strain the buckeye juice through bags.   The Creeks claim that the devil's shoestring poison used by the Yuchi floats on the water, thus passing away down stream,

Fig. 6.   Bundle of Poisonous Roots.

while the buckeye sinks and does better work.   It is probable, however, that neither method of poisoning the streams is used exclusively by these tribes, but that the people of certain districts favor one or the other method, according to the time of year and locality.   The flesh of the fish killed in this way is perfectly palatable.

It frequently happens that the poison is not strong enough to thoroughly stupefy the fish.   In such a case the men are at hand with bows and arrows, to shoot them as they flounder about trying to escape or to keep near the bottom of the pool.   The arrows used for shooting fish are different from those used in hunting.   They are generally unfeathered shafts with charred points, but the better ones are provided with points like cones made by pounding a piece of some flat metal over the end of the shaft (Fig. 4, a).   The men frequently go to the larger streams where the poison method would not be as effective, and shoot fish with these heavy tipped arrows either from the shores or from canoes.   Simple harpoons of cane whittled to a sharp point are used in the killing of larger fish which swim near the surface, or wooden spears with fire-hardened points are thrown at them when found lurking near the banks.

Formerly the Yuchi made use also of basket fish traps. These were quite large, being ordinarily about three feet or more in diameter and from six to ten feet in length. They were cylindrical in shape, with one end open and an indented funnel-shaped passageway leading to the interior. The warp splints of this indenture ended in sharp points left free. As these pointed inward they allowed the fish to pass readily in entering, but offered an obstruction to their exit. The other end of the trap was closed up, but the covering could be removed to remove the contents. Willow sticks composed the warp standards, while the wicker filling was of shaved hickory splints. The trap was weighted down in the water and chunks of meat were put in it for bait.

Gaff-hooks for fishing do not seem to have been used, according to the older men, until they obtained pins from the whites, when the Yuchi learned how to make fish hooks of them. Prior to this, nevertheless, they had several gorge-hook devices for baiting and snagging fish. A stick with pointed reverse barbs whittled along it near the end was covered with some white meat and drawn, or trolled, rapidly through the water on a line. When a fish swallowed the bait the angler gave the line a tug and the barbs caught the fish in the stomach. Another method was to tie together the ends of a springy, sharp-pointed splinter and cover the whole with meat for bait. When this gorge device was swallowed the binding soon disintegrated, the sharp ends being released killed the fish and held it fast. Lines thus baited were set in numbers along the banks of streams and visited regularly by fishermen.¶

POTTERY AND WORK IN CLAY.

The sedentary life of the Yuchi has given ample opportunity for the development of the art of making pottery. The coiled process is in vogue, but it may be remarked that the modern pots of these Indians are of a rather crude and unfinished form, which is probably traceable to deterioration in later years.

The process of manufacture of ordinary pots for domestic use is as follows. A fine consistent clay is selected and washed in a flat vessel to separate all grit and stones from it. Then lumps are rolled between the palms and elongated in the form of sticks. A flat piece, the size of the bottom of the desired pot, is made and the lengths or sticks of rolled clay are coiled around on this base and so built up until the proper height and form is obtained. Whatever decorations are to be added are now either produced by incision with a sharp stick or by impression with a stick or shell. The whole surface is afterwards scraped with a fresh-water mussel shell, *ctä^ngané* (Fig. 7), until the outside of the pot is smooth, and then, with the back of the shell, the scraped surface is rubbed to varying degrees of polish, or the hand may be used to give a dull lustre to the surface. The surface is moistened after the clay is dry

Fig. 7.   Shell Scraper.

and then rubbed until it assumes a fairly permanent polish. The pot is next allowed to dry for a few days out of the sunshine. Then it is baked near a fire. When several pots are being baked they are arranged in rows at a little distance from the fire on each side of it and turned at intervals. These pots become hard and brick-like and may be used directly over flames. If they are not baked they are used as household receptacles or dishes and not put near fire. This industry is entirely in the hands of women.

Pots, *sᵉä′cū dīdané,* 'earthen bowl,' or *dīdaⁿʹ* (Pl. III), which are made in general for ordinary domestic use are of several different shapes. The outlines shown in Fig. 8, *a, b, c, d, f* are the commonest. The low flat type, *a,* is ordinarily used for food dishes or receptacles for boiled beans and corn. They are usually about eight inches in diameter and three in height. A series of conventional straight lines running obliquely is often incised upon these vessels for the purpose of decoration, but w i t h o u t any known interpretation. Outline *b* shows the shape of a class of pots used for boiling vegetables. They are held upright by means of stones placed around the base. Their size is variable, ranging from those having a capacity of about three quarts to those holding five or six quarts. A little decoration, in the way of shallow impressions of semicircles, frequently appears near the rim of these boiling vessels to give, it is said, a decorative effect. The type represented by *c* is of an unusually rough and unfinished appearance and is said to be used to mix

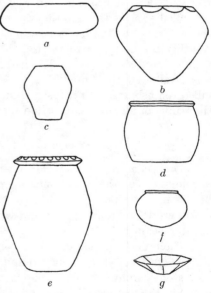

Fig. 8.   Outlines of Pots.

flour and dough in. The flat bottomed pot *d,* with a wide opening and almost straight sides, is the regular boiled corn soup pot which is made in different sizes according to the size of the family; they hold two quarts at least, and stand about the house or camp with food in them ready to be eaten cold or warm at any time. The two latter types do not bear on them any attempt at decoration whatever. Small cup-like vessels, *f*, not more than three or four inches broad, with rounded bottoms, are made for general utility in holding seeds and other objects. This is said to be the kind of clay vessel put in the grave with the body at burial.

One type of vessel, however, which is manufactured particularly for ceremonial purposes is invariably ornamented on a specially made portion about the rim.   This type of pot (Fig. 8, *e*, Plate III, Fig. 9) is used as the receptacle for the sacred concoctions at the annual ceremonies, the crescent-shaped impressions on the lip being said to represent the sun and moon, the former of which is the chief figure in mythology and the supernatural object of worship in the tribal ceremonies.   The height of these pots, two of which are used during the ceremonial events, is never less than twelve inches.   The crescent-like impressions are made with a bent-up twig when the clay is soft before being burnt.

The little platter *yáda dané* (Fig. 8, *g*, and Pl. III, Fig. 1), which is about three inches in diameter, is another form for a special purpose.   It is made for the use

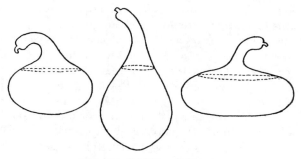

Fig. 9.   Outlines of Gourds.

of women who are in seclusion away from the main dwelling during their menstrual periods.   As these little trays are only used to carry food in to such women they are left unbaked.   When their function has been performed they are destroyed with other objects which have come into contact with women in this state.

It is noticeable in the above pottery forms, which are designed solely for domestic use, that no particular decoration is given them.   But where this does occur at all it is always on or near the rim and never on the body of the vessel. Specimen 5, Pl. III, and Fig. 8, *b*, have a curved impression surrounding the rim which is said to represent the moon.   The series of oblique scratches on specimen 8, Pl. III, had no meaning or name given them.

A question of origin naturally arises here, in relation to the pottery industry of this tribe, which seems to deserve mention at least.   The prominence of the gourd shape, or that of the pumpkin or squash, may have had some influence upon the development of forms in Yuchi pottery. The outline figures and the general appearance of pots suggest this question. The Yuchi themselves comment on the similarity between the shape of pots and pumpkins, and when asked about the form of this or that pot, the answer frequently is "It is like a pumpkin or gourd." The figures show how this similarity in form appears (Fig. 9). The similarity is further carried out by the smoothness of the body of the pots, and the diminishing diameter near the top. The drinking gourds found in use today, and the gourd receptacles used about the camps in the same way as pottery receptacles are similar to these in shape. The suspicion of this relationship between pottery forms and pumpkins or gourds was aroused by the replies given to questions which were asked in trying to find out whether the pottery shapes symbolized or represented anything else. For instance the bowls of wooden spoons are supposed to represent wolf ears.

It may be said of the modern Yuchi pottery forms that, according to the description given by Holmes[1], they bear more resemblance to those of the prehistoric Chesapeake-Potomac group in their prevalent gourd-like outline and lack of ornamentation on the body, than they do to the highly ornamented and complex forms of the Southern Appalachian group.

PIPES.—A large number of tobacco pipes of clay, sācū′ yūdᵋē′, 'earth pipes' (Fig. 11), were formerly made and used by the Yuchi. The variety in form shown by these pipes indicates that at an earlier time work in clay must have been a rather important activity with them. It seems that pipe making was, and is yet to a limited extent, practiced by the men. Clay is prepared in the manner described before for pots, and made into lengths about an inch in diameter. With a knife, cylinders of various lengths are cut out which are to be bent and hollowed into desired forms for the pipes. This shaping is done with the knife, the sides being shaved down round or square and the angles squared to suit the artisan's taste. The narrower end is twisted at right angles to the bowl to form the stem-holder. The knife is then used to gouge out and hollow the bowl. A small pointed stick (Fig. 10, a) is twisted into the stem end to make a hole for the stem, and when it has nearly reached the bowl cavity a small sharp twig is used to connect the two openings. After the exterior has been finished off with the knife the pipe is complete except for a cane or hollow twig stem. A piece of flint (Fig. 10, b) is often used to rub the pipe with and give it a polish, but generally none is thought necessary. The making

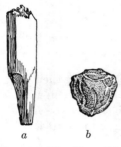

a   b

Fig. 10. Pipe Borer (a) and Polishing Stone (b)

---

[1] Twentieth Annual Report, Bureau of American Ethnology.

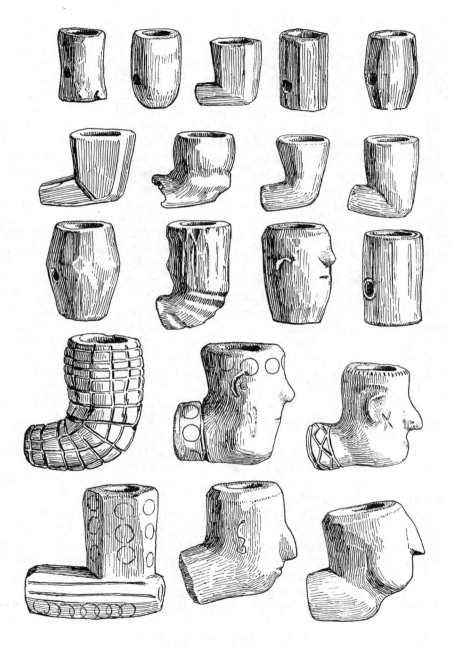

Fig. 11. Clay Pipes.

of effigy forms in pipes is mostly done by pressing and shaping with the fingers. The pipes are seldom baked, as this is gradually effected when they are lighted and put into use.

There seems to be no limit to the forms which different individuals give to the pipes they make. Personal taste appears to play an important part, however, within certain broad but traditional limits. The pipe forms observed seem to fall into a few different classes. It may be said that the commonest type is that having a stem-base at right angles to the bowl as illustrated in some of the examples shown in Fig. 11. These are rather small pipes, averaging a little over an inch in height. The bowls are squared, rounded or formed into hexagons. Another sort is barrel-shaped, also with different sectional forms and of the same small size as the first. These lack the stem-base, having the reed or cane stem inserted directly into the bowl. A third general type has a much larger and heavier form and suggests the catlinite calumet forms met with among the Plains Indians. The red color and carefully given polish of the specimens under discussion increase the apparent similarity between the two.

Effigy pipes (see Fig. 11) are favorites with the Yuchi and often show considerable skill on the part of the maker in imitating living forms. It is rather curious that those representing the human face never have eyes. The rings sometimes seen about the rim represent the Sun, who is the tutelary deity of the Yuchi. The frequent occurrence of the frog form in pipes is explained by the desire on the part of the men to emulate the Wind, a supernatural being who, according to the myth, used a frog for his pipe and a snake for the pipe-stem during one of his journeys.

A noticeable similarity in form appears between the modern pipes of the Yuchi and those found in the burial mounds of the Appalachian region, described by Holmes.[1]

The collections of objects from the mounds of Alabama, Georgia and Florida made by Mr. Clarence B. Moore[2] also contain many pipes in stone and earthenware which resemble the forms known to the modern Yuchi and illustrated in Fig. 11.

CLAY FIGURES.—The Yuchi men sometimes mould by hand pressure small figures of animals or parts of animals in clay. Just what part these clay figures play in their life it is hard to say. It would seem, however, that they are merely the product of an idle hour or are based on some esthetic motives. Where quite a little work is being done in clay by the women in making pots and by men who are fashioning smoking pipes, it would seem natural that some would idly try to shape, out of the unused material, figures

[1] Twentieth Report Bureau American Ethnology, Pls. cxxiv, cxxv, cxxvi.

[2] Journal of the Academy of Natural Sciences of Philadelphia, X, XI, XII, etc.

of objects familiar to them in their daily environment.   The figures of this sort are rather clumsy and naturally fragile since they are not baked.   The specimens on which this description is based are a crudely made lizard about eight inches long, several life-size frogs, and a cow's head several inches in height (Fig. 12).   Another correspondence between the modern Yuchi and the ancient inhabitants of the Southeast is to be found in these clay figures.   Mr. Moore in his archaeological explorations of the mounds of Volusia Co., Florida,[1] found numbers of rude clay figures among which some of the animal forms resemble the ones given here and obtained from the modern Yuchi.   The general technique in both modern and prehistoric specimens is similar.

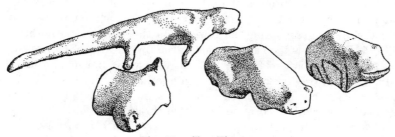

Fig. 12.   Clay Figures.

Finally it must be noted, in regard to the subject of pottery and work in clay, that this branch of native handicraft has undergone a great deterioration since the beginning of contact between the Yuchi and Europeans, and that the progress of decline in this, as in other arts, has been much more rapid in the last twenty-five years.   Most of the specimens described above were obtained by request, whereupon some were brought from remote districts where they may have been in actual use while others were fac-similes made for the occasion by reliable persons.

BASKET MAKING.

Another handicraft in the seemingly well-rounded industrial life of the Yuchi is basket making.   The women possess the knowledge of at least two processes of basket weaving; the checker work and the twilled.   The baskets in general are of two sorts.   One is a large rough kind made of hickory or oak splints not unlike the ordinary splint baskets made by the Algonkian tribes, with handles for carrying.   The other kind, in the manufacture of which cane rinds are chiefly employed, is distinctly characteristic of the Southeastern and Gulf area.   A collection of Yuchi baskets resembles those of the Choctaw or Chitimacha in general appearance and technique, although the Yuchi forms

[1] Collection of the Academy of Natural Sciences of Philadelphia.

obtainable today do not show as much diversity as the others.   In their present location, unfortunately, the Yuchi are handicapped by the lack of basket stuffs, while the other tribes still occupy territory where cane is abundant.   This may perhaps be the reason why we find the Yuchi comparatively deficient in variety of basket forms and weaves, when other tribes of the southern or Gulf area, as the Chitimacha, Attakapa and Choctaw, are considered.   The regular basket material is cane (*Arundinaria*).   For baskets of the common household storage type, intended as well for general domestic utility, the cane rind is the part used, as the outside is fine and smooth.   Splints from the inner portion of the cane stalk are employed in the construction of basket sieves and other coarser types.   The forms and outlines of common utility baskets, *dăstī'*, shown in Pl. IV, Figs. 1, 2, seem to resemble the common pottery forms in having the opening somewhat narrower than the bottom.   Another type of basket (Pl. IV, 5, 7) is the flat one used in the preparation of corn meal.   The largest of this class is two feet in breadth with walls not more than an inch or so high.   This tray basket is used with another, the sieve (Pl. IV, 6), which is also rather flat but not so much so as the former.   The bottom of the sieve basket is of open work.   Corn meal is sifted through this into the broad tray. Some idea of their respective proportions is given in Pl. IV, Figs. 5, 6.   The plan of the bottom of all of the basket forms described is rectangular in general, while that of the top is nearly round; at any rate, without angles.   The sides of the typical basket invariably slope inward with a rounding outline. This form, as can be readily seen, is largely determined by the nature of the weave.

Nearly all baskets of this region, with little exception, are manufactured by the twilled process of weaving.   It is noticeable that the bottom is customarily done in one pattern of twill and the sides in another variety of the same.   For example, we find one of the common forms like *a*, Fig. 13, woven at the bottom in the two over two under pattern, but when the turn for the sides is reached the vertical strands no longer run in twos but are separated, each simply alternating in crossing over two weft strands; the weft in its turn crossing four of the warp strands.   This mixture of technique seems to be a favorite thing with the Yuchi weavers.   Such purposeless variations in weave may be attributable to the rhythmic play motive which Dr. Boas has recently shown[1] to be prominent in the technique of many primitive tribes. An example is shown in Pl. IV, 2, 3, where a matting bottom (Fig. 13, *a*) is turned up into a woven side *b* with an over four under four weft.   The relationship between ordinary mats and baskets consequently appears to be a very close one.   At almost any stage in the process of mat weaving it appears

---

[1] Decorative Designs of Alaskan Needlecases, Proceedings of United States National Museum, Vol. xxxiv, p. 339-40.

that the operator can turn the strands up, fill in with a weft, and change the product into a basket.

Some examples of the varieties of twill which enter into the construction of mats and baskets are given in Fig. 13. The common diaper pattern may appear woven with double strands producing the variety shown in *a*. Baskets with

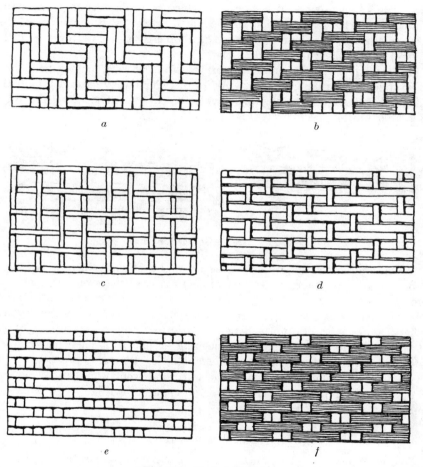

Fig. 13.   Basket Weaves.

this weave in the bottom and an over four under four on the sides are most characteristic, as will be seen. The basket sieves outlined before are woven in open mesh on the bottom, leaving open squares about one third of an inch square, *c*. Here the twill is the same, over two and under two as in Fig. 13, *a*, but done with narrower splints. The sides, however, of the basket sieve are filled in with weft strands going over two and under two, thus closing up the open spaces, as shown in *d*. The other cuts show some different varieties in which the number of warps crossed by the weft strands vary. Fig. 13, *b* is from the side of the work baskets in which the bottom appears as shown in *a*. The others, *e* and *f*, show the mat twill, the style that is oftenest found in the basket trays. The sides of the tray are changed to an over four under four twill as in *b*. The latter are held in the lap to catch the sifted corn meal that is shaken through the sieve. The use of the basket sieve, however, and this tray will be described in more detail later.

The basket border is commonly formed of a few warp lengths bent down and wrapped by a runner of cane. A row of twined weaving underneath this holds in place the warp strands that have to be cut off. The figure[1] illustrates this border finishing very well (Fig. 14).

Fig. 14.   Basket Border Finishing.

Intentional decorative designs seem to be almost entirely lacking in the baskets of today, and it is impossible to say whether or not they ever developed such designs. About the only decorative effect attempted seems to be the employment of cane splints of different shades of red and yellow in the weaving. Rather pretty diagonal patterns are in this way brought out, but they seem to have no assigned meaning or names. These patterns are quite evidently accidental in many instances, for the mere presence of one or two different colored splints in the warp and woof would work out into some geometrical pattern without any previous knowledge as to what this would be.

OTHER OCCUPATIONS.

WOOD WORKING.—The Yuchi men spend part of their time, when not engaged directly in procuring food, in manufacturing various useful articles out of wood. One form of knife, *yä^{n}lĭbŏ′*, 'knife bent,' used in whittling such objects, consists of a piece of iron curved at one end and sharpened on the side

---

[1] Taken from Mason's Aboriginal American Basketry in Report of U. S. National Museum, 1902.

after the fashion of a farrier's knife (Fig. 15). The handle part of the metal is bound around with cloth or skin to soften it for the grasp. The wood worker draws the knife towards himself in carving. Thus are made ladles, spoons, and other objects that come in handy about the house. Larger objects of wood are shaped not only by whittling with knives, but by burning. For instance dug-out canoes, *tcū sī'*, were made of cypress trunks hollowed out in the center by means of fire. As the wood became charred it was scraped away so that the fire could attack a fresh surface, and so on until the necessary part was removed.

It sometimes falls to the lot of women to help in the manufacture of certain wooden objects. One such case is to be seen in the hollowing out of the cavity of the corn mortar. After the man has sectioned a hickory log of the proper length and diameter, about 30 by 14 inches, he turns the matter over to several women of his household. They start a fire on top of the log, which is stood up on end. The fire is intended to burn away the heart of the log, so, to control its advance and to keep it going, two women blow upon it through hollow canes. By pouring water on the edge the fire is kept within bounds and confined to the center. As the wood becomes charred it is scraped away, as usual, with the shells of fresh water mussels.

No decorative effects are produced in wood carving nor is it likely that any particular development in technique was reached by the carvers in former times.

Fig. 15.
Crooked Knife.

PREPARING HIDES AND SEWING.—In preparing hides and skins for use the brains of animals are employed to soften and preserve them. Hides are placed over a log, one end of which is held between the knees while the other rests on the ground, and are then scraped with a scraping implement to remove the hair. The scraper, *tsᵉamē'satäné*, for this purpose is a round piece of wood about twelve inches long with a piece of metal set in edgewise on one side, leaving room for a hand grip on each end (Fig. 16). This implement resembles the

Fig. 16.   Scraper.

ordinary spokeshave more than anything else. A sharp edged stone is said to have taken the place of the iron blade in early times. Hides are finally thoroughly smoked until they are brown, and kneaded to make them soft and durable.

Sewing is done by piercing holes in the edges to be joined with an awl. Two methods of stitching are known, the simple running stitch and the overhand. The latter, on account of its strength, is, however, more commonly used. Sinew and deerskin thongs are employed for thread.

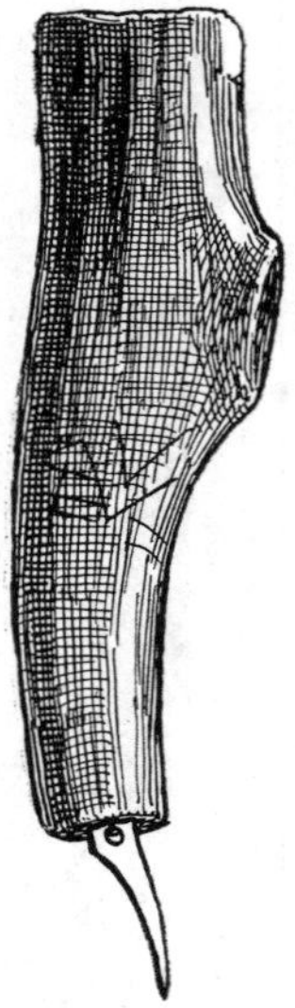

One specimen of awl, for sewing and basket making, consists of a piece of deer antler about six inches long into which a sharp pointed piece of metal is firmly inserted (Fig. 17). Bone is supposed to have been used for the point part before metal was obtainable. Several chevron-like scratches on the handle of this specimen are property marks.

A few knots and tying devices observed in use and on specimens, are given in Fig. 18. Softened deerskin thongs were employed for tying and binding purposes.

SHEET METAL WORK.—The manufacture of German silver ornaments, such as finger rings, earrings, bracelets, arm bands, breast pendants, head bands and brooches, seems to have been, for a long time, one of the handicrafts practiced by the Yuchi men. This art has now almost passed away among them and fallen into the hands of their Shawnee neighbors. The objects mentioned in the list were made of what appears to be copper, brass and zinc alloy. The metal was obtained from the whites, and then fashioned into desired shapes by cutting, beating, bending, and punching in the cold state.

Fig. 17. Awl.

The favorite method of ornamentation was to punch stars, circles, ovals, curves, scalloped lines, and crescents in the outer surface of the object. Sometimes the metal was punched completely through to produce

Fig. 18.   Tying Devices.

an open-work effect. Several pieces of metal were sometimes fastened together by riveting. Ornamental effects were added to the edges of objects by trimming and scalloping. It is also common to see fluting near the borders of bracelets and pendants. Judging from the technique in modern specimens, metal workers have shown considerable skill in working out their patterns. It is possible, moreover, that this art was practiced in pre-historic times with sheet copper for working material, in some cases possibly sheet gold, and that some of the ornaments, such as head bands, bracelets, arm bands and breast ornaments, were of native origin. Some of the ornamental metal objects will be described in connection with clothing.

BEADWORK.—Like many other Indian tribes the Yuchi adopted the practice of decorating parts of their clothing with glass beads which they obtained from the whites. Beadwork, however, never reached the development with them that it did in other regions. What there was of this practice was entirely in the hands of the women. There were two ways of using the beads for decoration. One of these was to sew them onto strips of cloth or leather, making embroidered designs in outline, or filling in the space enclosed by the outline to make a solidly covered surface. The other way was to string the beads on the warp threads while weaving a fabric, so that the design produced by arranging the colors would appear on both sides of the woven piece. For the warp and woof horse hair came to be much in use. Objects decorated in the first fashion were moccasins, legging flaps, breechcloth ends, garter bands, belt sashes and girdles, tobacco pouches and shoulder straps. The more complex woven beadwork was used chiefly for hair ornaments and neckbands.

The designs which appear in beadwork upon these articles of clothing are mostly conventional and some are symbolical with various traditional interpretations. They will be described later. It should be observed here, however, that there is some reason to suspect that the beadwork of this tribe has been influenced by that of neighboring groups where beadwork is a matter of more prominence. The removal of the Yuchi and other southeastern tribes from their old homes in Georgia and Alabama to the West threw them into the range of foreign influence which must have modified some characteristics of their culture.

STONE WORK.—Lastly we know, from the evidences of archeology, that at an early age the Yuchi, like the other Indians, were stone workers. All vestiges of this age, however, have passed beyond the recollection of the natives, so that nothing can be said first hand on the subject.

HOUSES.

As the native methods of house building have nearly all passed out of use some time ago, we have to depend upon descriptions from memory supplemented by observations made in the ceremonial camp where temporary shelters are made which preserve old methods of construction.

The dwelling house of the present-day Yuchi is like that of the ordinary white settler: a structure of squared or round notched logs, with a peak roof of home-made shingles and a door on one side. Windows may be present or not, according to the whim of the owner. The same is true of the fireplace, which may be an inside open grate at one end of the building, or a hearth in the middle of the room with smoke hole directly above. These houses show all possible grades of comfort and elaboration in their construction. Directly in front of the door it is customary to have a shade arbor raised where cooking is done. Here spare time is spent in comfortably lounging about while light occupations are carried on by various members of the family. Such a house is called *tsōlě'*, and may be, in its main idea, a survival of one form of original house. Bartram and other travelers who saw the southeastern Indians at an early date describe notched log houses among the Cherokee, so there is some possibility of the native origin of the simple square log house of the modern Yuchi and their neighbors the Creeks. Fortunately, however, we find in the work of Bartram[1] a fairly good, though short, description of the houses of the Yuchi as he saw them in the village on Chattahoochee river, Georgia, in 1791.

"The Uche town is situated on a vast plain, on the gradual ascent as we rise from a narrow strip of low ground immediately bordering on the river: it is the largest, most compact and best situated Indian town I ever saw; the habitations are large and neatly built; the walls of the houses are constructed of a wooden frame, then lathed and plastered inside and out with a reddish well tempered clay or mortar, which gives them the appearance of red brick walls, and these houses are neatly covered or roofed with cypress bark or shingles of that tree. The town appeared to be populous and thriving, full of youth and young children. . . ."

At certain times of the year when the people remove from these permanent houses and assemble at some convenient place for hunting, fishing or social intercourse they commonly make use of tents with an open structure nearby in which much unoccupied time is spent during both night and day. With some families this open-sided structure is merely a shade arbor, and no care seems to be given to its appearance. But with others it serves as the dwelling upon occasions and is fitted out and furnished with some semblance of permanent occupancy. During the annual tribal ceremony of the corn harvest, when the assemblage of families is largest, these structures may be best seen. The following descriptions of these temporary dwellings, in which are preserved earlier forms of architecture, are based upon observations made at such times.

---

[1] *Op. cit.*, p. 388.

To begin with, the camp shelters, as they are commonly called, are scattered irregularly about, in no wise forming a camp circle such as is found on the Plains or a camp square like that of the Chickasaw.[1] They are left standing after they have served once and are reoccupied by the owners when they return to the place where the ceremonial gatherings are held.

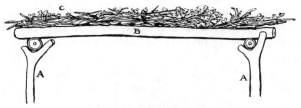

Fig. 19.   Roof Support.

The ground space covered by a lodge of this sort varies somewhat, but may be said to be in general about sixteen feet by eighteen.   The floor is simply the earth.   Branches of oak with the leaves compose the roof (Figs. 19, 20, C). Eight feet above the ground is a common height for this dense screen of leaves. The branches themselves are supported by cross poles (B) resting on stout

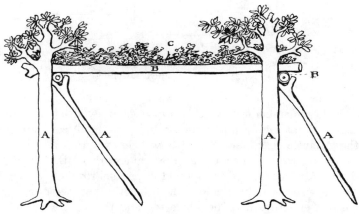

Fig. 20.   Roof Support.

horizontal end pieces or beams.   In the support of these beams, lodge builders employ different devices.   One of these, and perhaps the commonest, is the simple forked or crotched post (Fig. 19, A).   When trees happen to be handy, however, a modification has been observed in the roof support which shows a

---

[1] Cf. Journal of American Folk-Lore (1907), p. 50–58.

rather clever adaptation of the material at hand to suit the occasion.   In such a case standing trees take the place of sunken posts, and forked posts with the beams resting in the crotch are leaned against them, as in Fig. 20, A.

The general ground plan of these camp shelters is square (Fig. 21).   They usually stand east of the entrance to the tent (D).   In the center of the ground space (A) blankets, skins and other materials to make comfort are strewn, and here the people eat, lounge and sleep.   In one corner is a square storage scaffold or shelf (B) elevated about five feet above the ground.   This is floored with straight sticks resting upon cross pieces which in turn are supported by uprights in the floor.   On this scaffold is a heterogeneous pile of household untensils and property.   Ball sticks, weapons, baskets, clothing, harness, blankets and in fact nearly everything not in immediate use is all packed away here out of reach of dogs and children.   Out from under the roof to one side is the fireplace (C).   The diagram (Fig. 21) gives the ground plan of one of these lodges.

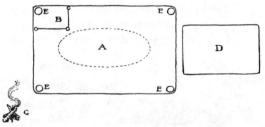

Fig. 21.   Plan of Yuchi Dwelling.

The Yuchi remember still another type of family dwelling house which seems to show that the common house type of the Algonkian tribes bordering the Atlantic coast farther north was known to the Yuchi as well. We are informed by the Yuchi that the framework of this type of house, *yū*, consisted of poles stuck in the ground in parallel rows at certain distances apart.   These were bent over and lashed together at the top, forming an arched passage underneath.   The whole top and the sides were then covered with strips of bark cut entire from cypress trees and attached in overlapping layers to the cross pieces connecting the upright poles.   Matting is also said to have been used as house covering material.   Such structures are commonly remembered to have been about ten feet high and about sixteen feet square on the ground.   The roof slabs were weighted down with halved logs secured at the ends to the framework.   The fireplace was in the center of the floor space.   It was excavated about six inches below the surface of the ground. A hole was left in the roof directly above the fireplace for the smoke to escape.

In the way of household furniture the Yuchi remember that beds, *tcu'fa*, used to consist of a framework of parallel sticks, supported by forked uprights, upon which skins were piled. These bench-like beds were ranged about the walls. Mats were suspended to form screens when desired.

Children were stowed away in hammock cradles when they were too young to walk. The hammock cradle is used very generally nowadays. It consists of a blanket stretched between two ropes. To keep the sides apart thwarts with notched ends are at the foot and head. The hammock is hung up out of doors from convenient trees, while in bad weather it is swung indoors from house posts or beams.

DOMESTIC UTENSILS.

In the preparation of food several kinds of wooden utensils are employed. The largest and perhaps the most important piece of household furniture of this sort was the mortar, *dīlá*, and pestle, *dīcä lá*. The mortar (Pl. III, Fig. 10, *a*) which is simply a log several feet high with the bark removed having a cavity about eight inches deep, seems, moreover, to be an important domestic fetish. We find that it is connected in some way with the growing up and the future prospects of the children of the family. It occupies a permanent position in the door yard, or the space in front of the house. Only one mortar is owned by the family and there is a strong feeling, even today, against moving it about and particularly against selling it. We shall see later that the navel string of a female child is laid away underneath the mortar in the belief that the presiding spirit will guide the growing girl in the path of domestic efficiency.

The pestle that goes with this utensil is also of wood (Pl. III, Fig. 10, *b*). Its length is usually about six feet. The lower end that goes into the cavity

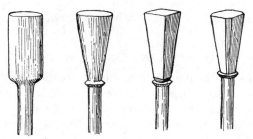

Fig. 22.   Pestle Tops.

of the mortar and does the crushing is rounded off. The top of the pestle is left broad, to act as a weight and give force to its descent. Several forms of carving are to be observed in these clubbed pestle tops which are presumably ornamental, as shown in the cuts (Fig. 22).

Spoons, *yáda ctīné*, showing some variation in size and relative proportions, are found commonly in domestic service. They are all made of wood, said to be maple. The size of these varies from six or seven to fourteen inches. The bowl is usually rather deep and is widest and deepest near the handle. The latter is squared and straight with a crook near the end upon which an ownership mark consisting of a few scratches or incisions is frequently seen. Pl. VI, 3 shows common spoons used in eating soup or boiled vegetables. This type is said to represent, in the shape of the bowl, a wolf's ear and to be patterned after it.

Wooden paddle-shaped pot stirrers, *cadĭ'*, are nearly always to be seen where cooking is going on. They vary greatly in size and pattern. Ordinarily the top is simply disk-shaped. The use of the stirrer comes in when soup and vegetables are being boiled, to keep the mess from sticking to the pot. (See models in Fig. 36, *b*.)

Gourds, *tä'mbactū'*, of various shapes are made use of about the house in many different ways. They are easily obtained and require little or no

labor to fit them for use. As drinking cups, general receptacles and dippers they come in very handy. A common drinking ladle is shown in Figure 23. Besides these utensils, of course, baskets, mats, and pots, which have been dealt with already, figure prominently in the household economy. Pots are used chiefly as cooking vessels and receptacles from which prepared food is eaten. Baskets are commonly used for storing things away, for carrying purposes and for the keeping of ornaments, trinkets, small utensils and other personal effects. The several specialized forms, the riddle, or basket sieve, and the fan, or flat basket tray, are, as has been mentioned, used directly in the preparation of corn for food. The part they play will be described in more detail in another place.

Fig. 23.
Drinking Gourd.

FOOD AND ITS PREPARATION.

FIRE MAKING.—In the preparation of most vegetable and animal products for consumption fire is an indispensable agent. It is also procured for ceremonial purposes. To obtain it the Yuchi claim that originally two pieces of stone were struck together, either two pieces of flint or a piece of flint and a piece of quartz or pyrites. In the annual tribal ceremony this method is preserved yet. Two persons are ordinarily required in producing fire, one to do the striking, the other to hold the bed of fire material into which the spark is projected when obtained. A single individual might succeed very well, but two together obtain fire much more quickly. Even then the operation often takes fifteen minutes or more. It is likely, however, that the manipulators were already out of practice when the method passed out of common use.   It is nowadays admitted that the town chief who strikes the spark at the annual ceremony is greatly worried at this time over the ultimate result of his efforts.   It takes him about twenty minutes to secure a flame.

The method, as observed on several ceremonial occasions, is as follows: the flint, *yät ᵋä dawoné*, is held between the thumb and forefinger of the right hand with a small piece of punk material, *tciñgᵋǒ'*, alongside of it.   This punk appears to be a very close-pored fungus.   In his left hand he holds the striker.   The helper stands by, holding a curved tray of hickory bark heaped up with decayed wood, *sämbī'*, which has been dried and reduced to powder (Fig. 24).   The chief operator then strikes the two stones together,

Fig. 24.   Tinder Tray.

and when several good sparks have been seen to fly, a moment is given to watching for evidence that one has been kept alive in the punk.   If the spark smoulders in this it is gently transferred to the tinder in the bark tray.   From this moment the responsibility rests with the helper.   He begins to sway the tinder very gradually from side to side and gauges his movements by the thin wisp of smoke that arises from the smouldering bed.   After a few minutes, if things go well, the smoke increases and the helper becomes more energetic.   The climax is reached when from the dried wood tinder-bed a little flame springs up.   Small twigs are piled on and then larger ones until the blazing mass can be safely deposited beneath a pile of firewood.   Nowadays at any rate, the fire-producing materials, flint and punk, are a part of the town chief's sacred paraphernalia and he has the prerogative of manipulating them.   A piece of steel is more often used as a sparker in the modern operation, as it is more effective.

The most convenient fireplace arrangement is to have a large, not too dry backlog with the fire maintained along one side according to the number of pots to be heated.   When the backlog burns away in one place the fire is moved to another, or the log itself is pushed along.

As to the origin of fire we find here the common American explanation. It is believed to have been stolen, by the mythical trickster Rabbit, from a people across the waters and brought by him to the Yuchi.

FOODS.—Foodstuffs in which corn or maize is the principal ingredient should be mentioned first in this connection. In its various forms corn has always been the staple article of diet in the region inhabited by these Indians, while at certain times of the year game, fish and fruits have supplemented the daily menu. Pumpkins, potatoes, beans, melons and squashes rank next in the list of cultivated plant foods. The variety of corn best known seems to have been what is commonly called flint corn

The simplest way of preparing corn for use is to boil it or roast it in the ear and eat it directly from the cob. There is, however, only a certain time of the year in which this can be done and that is when the crop has matured, after the supernatural powers had been propitiated and the bodies of the people purified by ceremonies to be treated later under the subject of religion. One of the chief articles of diet is *tsō'ci*, a kind of corn soup.[1] To make this the grains of corn, when dry, are removed from the cob and pounded in the mortar until they are broken up. These grits and the corn powder are then scooped out of the mortar and boiled in a pot with water. Wood ashes from the fire are usually added to it to give a peculiar flavor much to the native taste. Even powdered hickory nuts, or marrow, or meat may be boiled with the soup to vary its taste. It is commonly believed, as regards the origin of this favorite dish, that a woman in the mythical ages cut a rent in the sky through which a peculiar liquid flowed which was found to be good to eat. The Sun then explained its preparation and use, from which fact it was called *tsō'ci*, inferably 'sun fluid.'

A kind of corn flour, *tsukhá*, is made by pounding up dried corn in the mortar. At intervals the contents of the mortar are scooped up and emptied into the sieve basket. The operator holds a large basket tray in her lap and over it shakes and sifts the pounded corn until all the grits and the finer particles have fallen through. According to the desired fineness or coarseness of the flour she then jounces this tray until she has the meal as she wants it, all the chaff having blown away. The meal, being then ready to be mixed into dough, is stirred up with water in one of the pottery vessels. In the meantime a large clean flat stone has been tilted slantwise before the embers of a fire. When the dough is right it is poured out onto this stone and allowed to bake. These meal cakes constitute the native bread, *kánlo*. Berries are thought to improve the flavor and are often mixed in with the dough. Besides corn the Yuchi preserve the knowledge of a variety of foods some of which are still commonly used. Hickory nuts, *yʌ'*, were commonly stored away for use in the following manner. They were pounded and then

---

[1] The common name for this corn soup is *sofki*, the Creek term, which has come now to be widely used for the dish among both Indians and whites.

boiled in water until a milk-like fluid was obtained. This after being strained was used as a beverage or as a cooking ingredient.

Almost any bird, animal or fish that was large enough to bother with was used as food. The names and varieties of such have been already given. The flesh of game mammals, birds, *kändī'*, and fish, *cū*, was roasted or broiled on a framework of green sticks resting on cross pieces which were supported on forked uprights over the fire. The device was simply a stationary broiling frame. When large hauls of fish were made, by using vegetable poison in streams in the manner described, or more game was taken than was needed for immediate use, it is said that the surplus flesh was artificially dried over a slow smoky fire or in the sun, so that it could be laid away against the future. Crawfish, *tcatsá*, were very much liked and quantities of them were also treated for preservation in the above manner.

Wild fruits and nuts in their proper seasons added variety to the comparatively well supplied larder of the natives. Berries, *yäbä'*, were gathered and dried to be mixed with flour or eaten alone. Wild grapes, *cä*, were abundant. The Indians are said to have preserved them for use out of season by drying them on frames over a bed of embers until they were like raisins, in condition to be stored away in baskets.

Salt, *dábī*, was used with food except during the annual tribal ceremony and for a short time before it, when it was tabooed in the same sense as corn or intercourse with women. It was obtained from river banks in certain places, but, on the whole, was rather a rare article with the Yuchi.

Meals were seldom eaten at regular times. Since food of some sort was nearly always over the fire or ready to eat, the different members of the family, or even outsiders, partook of what they wanted whenever they felt inclined. At least once a day, however, one good meal would usually be prepared for all.

The food supply of the Indians of the fertile Southeast, regulated by their forethought in preserving grain and flesh, seems to have been on the whole, fairly constant and abundant. Accordingly we do not expect to find them making use of matter that is not acceptable to the average human taste, such, for instance, as insects, larvæ, and small reptiles. They did, however, and do today, find the raw entrails of the larger mammals and their contents to be much to their liking, esteeming the substance a delicacy.

A more extensive list of special vegetable foods could hardly be gotten from the Yuchi today as they are out of their original habitat, and have discontinued the use of wild plants for some time.

In connection with animal foods it should be remembered that there were numerous clans having particular animals for their totems, and that there existed for each clan the taboo of killing or eating the particular animal which bore the form of its totem.

Dress and Ornament.

For a people living in quite a warm climate the Yuchi, as far back as they have any definite knowledge, seem to have gone about rather profusely clothed, but the descriptions obtained refer only to a time when the white traders' materials had replaced almost entirely the native products.

A bright colored calico shirt was worn by the men next to the skin. Over this was a sleeved jacket reaching, on young men, a little below the waist, on old men and chiefs, below the knees. The shirt hung free before and behind, but was bound around the waist by a belt or woolen sash. The older men who wore the long coat-like garment had another sash with tassels dangling at the sides outside of this. These two garments, it should be remembered, were nearly always of calico or cotton goods, while it sometimes happened that the long coat was of deerskin. Loin coverings were of two kinds; either a simple apron was suspended from a girdle next the skin before and behind, or a long narrow strip of stroud passed between the legs and was tucked underneath the girdle in front and in back, where the ends were allowed to fall as flaps. Leggings of stroud or deerskin reaching from ankle to hip were supported by thongs to the belt and bound to the leg by tasselled and beaded garter bands below the knee. Deerskin moccasins covered the feet. Turbans of cloth, often held in place by a metal head band in which feathers were set for ornament, covered the head. The man's outfit was then complete when he had donned his bead-decorated side pouch, in which he kept pipe, tobacco and other personal necessities, with its broad highly embroidered bandolier. The other ornaments were metal breast pendants, earrings, finger rings, bracelets and armlets, beadwork neckbands and beadwork strips which were fastened in the hair. The women wore calico dresses often ornamented on the breast, shoulders, and about the lower part of the skirt with metal brooches. Necklaces of large round beads, metal earrings and bracelets were added for ornament, and upon festive or ceremonial occasions a large, curved, highly ornate metal comb surmounted the crown of the head. From this varicolored ribbons dangled to the ground, trailing out horizontally as the wearer moved about. The woman's wardrobe also included an outside belt, decorated with bead embroidery, short leggings, and moccasins at times.

The above articles of clothing, as can quite readily be seen, are largely of modern form if not of comparatively modern origin. However, owing to the fact that no period is remembered by the Yuchi going back of the time when these things were in use, we are left to our own resources in trying to determine which of them were native and which of them were borrowed from outsiders.

If we are warranted in judging by the material used and by the form of decoration which is given them, it would seem that among the garments described, leggings, breechcloths, moccasins and perhaps shirts and turbans at least were of native type. The same, furthermore, might be said of some forms of the metal ornaments, ornamented necklaces, hair ornaments, sashes and knee bands. So far as is now known, the decorative art of the Yuchi is almost exclusively confined to the latter articles, and it may be that the antiquity of the decorative designs is paralleled by that of the objects which carry them. Reference is made in myths to the turban, woman's skirt, man's sash and carrying pouch with its broad bandolier in connection with one of the supernatural beings, Wind. The peculiar form of these articles as worn by him then gave the motive for the conventional decorations which are still put on such articles by the Yuchi. This, however, is to be dealt with more fully under the next heading.

The bright colored calico shirt worn next to the skin was called *gōci bilané*, 'what goes around the back;' and was provided with buttons and often a frill around the collar and at the wrists. The outer garment, *gōci stalé*, 'over the back,' of calico also, was more characteristic. This had short sleeves with frilled cuff bands which came just above the frills of the under shirt, thereby adding to the frilled effect. A large turn-down collar bordered with a frill which ran all around the lapels down the front and about the hem, added further to this picturesque effect, and a great variety of coloring is exhibited in the specimens which I have seen. The long skirted coat, *gocī stale$^\varepsilon$ä'*, worn by the old men, chiefs and town officials, was usually white with, however, just as many frills. An old specimen of Cherokee coat is shown in Pl. V, 1, which shows very well the sort of coat commonly worn by the men of other southeastern tribes as well as the Yuchi. The material used is tanned buckskin with sewed-on fringe corresponding to the calico frills in more modern specimens. It is said that as the men became older and more venerable, they lengthened the skirts of their coats. A sash commonly held these coats in at the waist.

The breechcloth, *gontsoné^n* (Pl. V, Fig. 2), was a piece of stroud with decorated border, which was drawn between the legs and under the girdle before and behind. The flaps, long or short as they might be, are said to have been decorated with bead embroidery, but none of the specimens preserved show it.

Leggings, *to$^\varepsilon$o'*, were originally of deerskin with the seam down the outside of the leg arranged so as to leave a flap three or four inches wide along the entire length. The stuff was usually stained in some uniform color. In the latter days, however, strouding, or some other heavy substance such as broadcloth, took the place of deerskin, and the favorite colors for this were black, red and blue. The outside edge of the broad flap invariably bore some decoration, in following out which we find quite uniformly one main idea. By means of ribbons of several colors sewed on the flap a series of long parallel lines in red, yellow, blue and green are brought out. The theme is said to represent sunrise or sunset and is one of the traditional decorations for legging flaps. A typical specimen is shown in Plate V, 3. The legging itself reaches from the instep to the hip on the outer side where a string or thong is attached with which to fasten it to the belt for support.

The moccasin, *detᵉä'*, still in use (Pl.V,4, and Fig. 25), is made of soft smoked deerskin. It is constructed of one piece of skin. One seam runs straight up the heel. The front seam begins where the toes touch the ground and runs along the instep. At the ankle this seam ends, the uppers hanging loose. The instep seam is sometimes covered with some fancy cloth. Deerskin thongs are fastened at the instep near the bend of the ankle with which to bind the moccasin fast. The thongs are wound just above the ankle and tied in front.

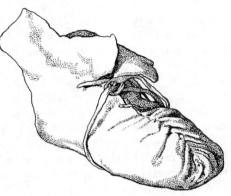

Fig. 25.   Man's Moccasin.

Sometimes a length of thong is passed once around the middle of the foot, crossing the sole underneath, then wound once around the ankle and tied in front. This extra binding going beneath the sole is employed generally by those whose feet are large, otherwise the shoe hangs too loose. The Osages, now just north of the Yuchi, employ this method of binding the moccasins quite generally, but the moccasin pattern is quite different. The idea, however, may be a b o r r o w e d one. Yuchi moccasins have no trailers or instep flaps or lapels, the whole article being extremely plain. It seems that decoration other than the applications of red paint is quite generally lacking.

The turban, *to cĭné*, seems to have been a characteristic piece of head gear in the Southeast. The historic turban of the Yuchi was a long strip of calico or even heavier goods which was simply wound round and round the head and had the end tucked in under one of the folds to hold it. The turban cloth was of one color, or it could have some pattern according to personal fancy. Plumes or feathers were in the same way stuck in its folds for the artistic effect. That some head covering similar to the turban was known in Precolumbian times seems probable inasmuch as a myth mentions that Rabbit, when he stole the ember of fire from its keepers, hid it in the folds of his head dress.

The sashes, *gágódĭ kwené*, 'the two suspended from the body' (Pl. V, 5, 6, Pl. VI, 7, 8), worn by men, are made of woolen yarn. The simplest of these consists merely of a bunch of strands twisted together and wrapped at the ends. A loose knot holds the sash about the waist. But the characteristic sash of the southeastern tribes, and one much in favor with the Yuchi, is

more complex in its makeup, and quite attractive in effect, the specimens
I have seen being for the most part knitted. The sashes of the Yuchi seem
to be uniformly woven with yarn of a dark red color. Some specimens,
however, show an intermixture of blue or yellow, or both. The main feature
is a dark red ground for the white beads which are strung on the weft.
Figures of triangles and lozenges or zigzags are attractively produced
by the white beaded outlines and the conventional design produced is
called 'bull snake.' The sash is tied about the waist so that the fixed
tassels fall from one hip and the tassels at the knotted end depend from
the other. Customarily the tassels reach to the knee. The sash is a
mark of distinction, to a certain extent, as it was only worn in former times
by full-grown men. Nowadays, however, it is worn in ball games and upon
ceremonial occasions by the participants in general, though only as regalia.

The woven garters, *tsē tsA*ⁿ' (Pl. VI, 3), or *godē' kwené*, 'leg suspender,'
should be described with the sash, as their manner of construction and their
conventional decoration is the same. The garters or knee bands are several
inches in width. They are commonly knitted, while the tassels are of plaited
or corded lengths of yarn with tufts at the ends. Here the general form and
colors of the decorative scheme are the same as those of the sash. The function of the knee band seems to be, if anything, to gather up and hold the slack
of the legging so as to relieve some of the weight on the thong that fastens it
to the belt. The tasseled ends fall half way down the lower leg.

Rather large pouches, *lätī'*, two of which are ordinarily owned by each
man as side receptacles, are made of leather, or goods obtained from the whites,
and slung over the shoulder on a broad strap of the same material. It has
already been said that various articles were thus carried about on the person:
tobacco and pipe, tinder and flint, medicinal roots, fetishes and undoubtedly
a miscellaneous lot of other things. The shoulder strap is customarily
decorated with the bull snake design by attaching beads, or if the strap be
woven, by weaving them in. There seems to be a variety in the bead decorations on the body of the pouch. Realistic portrayals of animals, stars,
crescents and other objects have been observed, but the realistic figure of
the turtle is nearly always present either alone or with the others. The
turtle here is used conventionally in the same way that the bull snake is
used as the decorative theme on sashes and shoulder strap, that is, in
imitation of the mythical being Wind who went forth with a turtle for
his side pouch. In Pl. IX. Fig. 5, one of the chief ornamental designs is
reproduced.

The next ornamental pieces to be described are the neckbands, *tsūtso*ⁿ *la'*,
'bead band' (Pl. VI, 5, 6), worn by men. These are usually an inch in width
and consist of beads strung on woof of horse hair; each bead being placed
between two of the warps. Beadwork of this sort is widely used by the

neighboring Sauk and Fox and Osage and it may be that we are dealing here with a borrowed idea. Not only the idea of the neckband, but also many of the decorative motives brought out on it, may possibly be traceable to Sauk and Fox or other foreign sources. The religious interests of the Yuchi are largely concerned with supernatural beings residing in the sky and clouds, so we find many of the conventional designs on these neckbands interpreted as clouds, sun, sunrise and sunset effects, and so on. Animal representations, however, are sparingly found, while on the other hand representations of rivers, mountains, land, and earth, are quite frequent. On the whole it seems that most of the expression of the art of these Indians is to be found on their neckbands and the hair ornaments. In thus bearing the burden of conventional artistic expression in a tribe, the neckband of the Yuchi is something like the moccasin of the Plains, the pottery of the Southwest and the basketry of California.

Fastened in the hair near the crown and falling toward the back, the men used to wear small strips of beadwork, *tsū'tsetsĭ'*, 'little bead' (Pl. VI, 4), avowedly for ornament. They were woven like the neckband on horse hair or sinew with different colored beads. One which I collected is about eight inches long and one half an inch wide, having three-fold dangling ends ornamented with yarn. The designs on these ornaments are representative of topographical and celestial features.

A woman's belt, *wänté gahò'ndē kwené*, 'goes around woman's waist', is shown (Pl. VI, 1). The belts were of leather or trade cloth and had bead embroidery decorations representing in general the same range of objects as the neckbands and hair ornaments. Such belts were usually about two

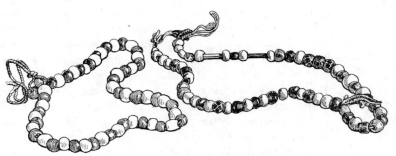

Fig. 26.   Women's Necklaces.

inches wide. Women's dresses, *noⁿgᵉā'*, will not be described, as they present nothing characteristic or original. Most women are found with strings of large round blue beads about their necks (Fig. 26). It is stated that necklaces of this sort have something to do with the fertility of women.

The ornaments which were made of silver alloy beaten and punched in the cold state are exceedingly numerous and varied. The use of such objects has been very general among the Indians and a general borrowing and interchanging of pattern and shape seems to have gone on for some time during the historic period. No particularly characteristic forms are found among the Yuchi except perhaps in the breast pendants, which are generally crescent shaped, and the men's head bands and the women's ornamental combs. Some of these objects deserve description.

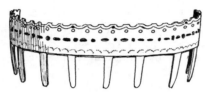

Fig. 27.   Ornamental Comb.

Fig. 27 shows one of the combs. The narrow band of metal is decorated with punched-in circles, ovals and toothed curves. The teeth are cut out of another strip of metal which is riveted on. The upper edge of the comb is scalloped. Women's bracelets are shown in Fig. 28, with similar ornamentation

Fig. 28.   Bracelets.

on the body, and grooves near the edges to render its shape firm. The rings, gōmpadï'né, and earrings (Fig. 29) need no description. Hardly any two are alike.

We have evidence in the myths that robes, ʌntcwá, or hides of animals,

Fig. 29.   Finger Rings.

as the name implies, were worn by the men over their shoulders. The case referred to mentions bear and wildcat skins used in this manner and it is also to be inferred that two different branches of the tribe were characterized by the wearing of bear and wildcat skins robes.

The men furthermore affect the fan, *wetcá*, 'turkey' (Pl. VII, 9), of wild turkey tail feathers. The proper possession of this, however, is with the older men and chiefs who spend much of their time in leisure. They handle the fan very gracefully in emphasizing their gestures and in keeping insects away. During ceremonies to carry the fan is a sign of leadership. It is passed to a dancer as an invitation to lead the next dance. He, when he has completed his duty, returns it to the master of ceremonies who then bestows it upon someone else. The construction of the fan is very simple, the quills being merely strung together upon a string in several places near the base (Fig. 30).

The Yuchi men as a rule allow the hair to grow long all over the head until it reaches the neck. It is then cropped off even all around and worn parted in the middle. The portrait of the old man (Pl. I) shows this fairly well. Something is usually bound about the forehead to keep the hair back from the face; either a turban, silver head band or strip of some kind. The beadwork hair ornaments used to be tied to a few locks back of the crown. Some of the older men state that a long time ago the men wore scalp locks and

Fig. 30.   Feather Attachment of Fan.

roached their hair, removing all but the comb of hair along the top of the crown, in the manner still practiced by the Osage. Men of taste invariably keep the mustache, beard and sometimes the eyebrows from growing by pulling them out with their finger nails. The hair was formerly trimmed by means of two stones. The tresses to be cut were laid across a flat stone and were then sawed off, by means of a sharp-edged stone, to the desired length.

The women simply part their hair in the middle, gathering it back tightly above the ears and twisting it into a knot or club at the back of the neck. The silver combs, already described, are placed at the back near the top of the head.

Face painting, as we shall see, is practiced by both men and women for certain definite purposes. There are four or five patterns for men and they indicate which of two societies, namely the Chief or the Warrior society, the wearer belongs to. These patterns are shown in Pl. X, and will be described in more detail later on. Although the privilege of wearing certain of these patterns is inherited from the father, young men are not, as a rule, entitled to use them until they have been initiated into the town and can take a wife.

Face painting is an important ceremonial decoration and is scrupulously worn at ceremonies, public occasions and ball games. A man is also decorated with his society design for burial.

The only use ever made of paint in the case of women seems to have been to advertise the fact that they were unmarried. Women of various ages are now, however, observed with paint, and it is generally stated that no significance is attached to it. One informant gave the above information in regard to the past use of paint among women and thought that to wear it was regarded then as a sign of willingness to grant sexual privileges. The woman's pattern consists simply of a circular spot in red, about one inch across, on each cheek (Pl. X, Fig. 4). A few other objects of personal ornament which are, however, functionally more ceremonial will be described when dealing specifically with the ceremonies.

DECORATIVE ART AND SYMBOLISM.

Something has already been said about decorative designs in the description of clothing, but the designs themselves and the general subject of art deserve a little attention. As regards the artistic expression of this tribe it seems that, in general, special conventional decorations symbolizing concrete objects are confined to a few articles of clothing such as neckbands, sashes, hair ornaments, leggings and carrying-pouches. The whole field is permeated with a strong religious significance. Decorations of a like sort with a still more emphatic religious meaning are found on pottery, though rarely, as well as on other objects. Besides this we find occasional attempts, on the part of the men, to make realistic pictures of familiar objects by means of pigments on paper, bark or skin, not to mention the fashioning of a few crude representations in plastic material. Considering, however, the part that conventional decoration plays in the present case, it seems to outweigh the importance of pictorial art. It must be admitted, though, that this supposition is founded entirely on the consideration of modern material, and, as there appears to be no way of going back of this for an insight into earlier stages, the only course is to treat it as a native feature. A suspicion regarding the foreign origin of Yuchi ornamentation has already been mentioned. We must also reckon with considerable deterioration resulting from contact with the whites.

Lacking, then, the ability to deal with Yuchi art in its definitely pure state we shall undertake the consideration of some decorative designs on clothing as representing the most specialized and characteristic surviving forms. Some of these are simple conventional geometrical patterns which are used with variation by different individuals and often regarded as religious symbols. For instance, we find the conventional bull snake pattern on sashes, garters, neckbands and shoulder straps, with a religious significance attached to it. Inasmuch as the Wind on one of his excursions made use of bull snakes for his sash, garters and shoulder strap and was highly successful in his undertaking, the emulation of this great being is sought after by human beings when they decorate their sashes, garters and shoulder straps with the symbolic bull snake design.[1] The same emulative motives are to be found in the frog

---

[1] The likelihood that the snake design was predominant in the decoration of shoulder straps and sashes of most of the southeastern tribes is to be inferred from the frequency with which this design, to the exclusion of others, appears in the portraits of Creeks, Seminole and Cherokee published by McKenney and Hall (History of the Indian Tribes of North America, 3 vols., 1848–50).

effigy pipes and in the turtle design which is common on the side pouches (Pl. IX. Fig. 5).

Other patterns lack, so far as is known, any religious associations, being merely conventional decorative representations of familiar natural objects. In this category we find patterns of mountains, clouds, rivers, the moon, sun, milky way, and rainbow, while representations of such living forms as the centipede and the bull snake are also met with. The greatest variety of patterns showing minor differences and bearing the same interpretation seem to be those representing sky and cloud effects. The religious interest of the Yuchi in the upper world of the sky may have influenced them in their taste for celestial symbols. In this connection it should be remembered that they regard themselves as the offspring of the sun and point to that orb as the tribal sign in gesture talk. It was remarked by one of the men who supplied the specimens illustrated here, that some years ago when the Yuchi were more given to roving about the plains for game they were distinguished among the Osage, Sauk, Pawnee and other tribes encountered, by the predominance of cloud, sky, sun and moon designs shown in their beadwork neckbands. In fact, the decorative motives seem to be of a more or less fixed tribal nature. No symbols for abstract ideas, as for example those of the Arapaho for thought and good luck, have been found.

In depicting objects and in conventional patterns naturally the outlines give the chief character to the figure, though colors have their conventional uses. Blue represents sky or water, dark blue, the sky at night, and white or yellow, light or illumination. Green represents vegetation. Brown, earth or sand, and red, earth and fire. As among many tribes of North America, colors are furthermore associated with the cardinal points by the Yuchi.

> kōda^{n}ǰá, north; hitsʌ$^{n\prime}$, green or blue.
> ǰaka^{n}ǰá, east; yaká, white.
> wä′ ǰa, south; tcaɫá, red.
> ǰa^{n}ǰá, west; ispī′, black.

Of these, two carry the symbolism further. The east and its whiteness signify the propitious, the west and black stand for the unpropitious, while red is symbolical of war and turbulence. These concepts, at least the black west and the white east, are undoubtedly connected with day and night.

In different accounts the colors going with the cardinal points vary somewhat. It appears that no fixed symbolism is maintained but that the idea of color in connection with the points is general but variable. The same tendency seems to be found in other tribes, which would explain the conflicts which are often recorded.

The illustrations given here were mostly made from specimens secured from the Indians and the interpretations are those offered by their makers. In some cases, however, patterns were remembered by Indians but no actual specimens showing them could be obtained. Pigment representations in color were then made by the Indians of a few designs which were familiar to them but out of use, and the interpretations were secured at the same time as the sketches. Other designs were copied from specimens which could not be obtained. Pl. VIII, Fig. 8 is a general pattern representing the bull snake, *canká*, on earth or sand. It was done in pigment and said to be intended for use on shoulder straps of pouches, garters or sashes. Fig. 7 also shows a pattern of the bull snake design for similar use; the body material here is supposed to be of some white cloth and the red, yellow and blue outlines are to be produced by sewing the beads on or weaving them singly in the fabric. Fig. 6 is an actual design taken from a pair of woven garters. The white beads are woven in the fabric and the whole also symbolizes the bull snake. Fig. 2 is a pattern representing the centipede, *totce^{n}gäné*. It was done in pigments and is intended for use on beadwork neckbands. Figs. 3 and 4 are both from specimens of beadwork neckbands and show three-color conventionalizations of the centipede. Fig. 5 represents the same with the difference that the legs are shown in the outside marginal row. Fig. 1 and Pl. IX Fig. 4, show mountain designs seen on breechcloth flaps, blankets, and belts, and used also on neckbands. This is called *s^{ε}ä′yaboha pē′^{ε}e^n*, 'many crooked mountains.' Pl. VIII. Fig. 9, is a pattern, *tsē^{ε}ä′*, river, taken from a neckband representing a river, in blue, flowing through arid country, indicated by the brown ground color. Fig. 15 is another neckband design showing the same idea with a little variation in color. Fig. 14 is a hair ornament representing likewise a river flowing through a fertile prairie land. In Fig. 13 is a pigment pattern for belt, shoulder strap or neckband. It represents an otter, according to its well-known habit, sliding down the bank of a stream into the water which is represented by the blue area. The red portion shows the muddy bank. Fig. 12 is taken from a beadwork neckband and shows the milky way, *tsené yūctä^n*, 'dog's trail,' in white, as seen on a starlight night. The dark blue represents the sky at night and the white beads in it are stars. Fig. 11 shows the design on a woman's belt done in beads and cloth appliquée. The whole represents the breaking up of storm clouds, showing glimpses of the blue sky in between the cloud banks. Fig. 16 is from a beadwork necklace and represents a bright sky with various kinds of cumulus clouds which are shown in the different shaped rectangles. Fig. 10 is another neckband design representing the rainbow, *yū^{ε}ä′* or *wet^{ε}ä′*. Fig. 17, taken from a neckband, is similar in content to Fig. 16, showing cumulus clouds.[1] The right angle L represents the moon. Figs. 18 and 19 are neckband and hair ornament designs representing different sunrise or sunset effects, *tson$_A$^{n}′*.

One informant gave the additional name of "boxes" to the rectangles.

Fig. 20 is a variation of the idea represented in Fig. 17, showing also the moon symbol. This was taken from a beadwork neckband. Fig. 21, also a neckband idea, is uniform red representing the glow of sunset in the sky, and is called *hopoⁿlé tcalála,* 'sky red all over.' Figs. 22 and 23 are beadwork design elements also representing sunrise or sunset amid clouds.

The most characteristic and important example of religious symbolism is to be found in the public area or town square of Yuchi town where the ceremonies are performed and tribal gatherings take place. Although this will be described and figured further on under another heading (see Pl.XI), it deserves mention here. The town square itself, with its three lodges on the north, south and west, symbolized the rainbow. The natural coloring of the brown earth floor of the square, the green brush roofs of the lodges, the gray ashes of the fire in the center and the red of the flames formed altogether an enormous ashes, earth and vegetation painting, if such an expression might be used, which was the tribal shrine. The colors of this town square altar corresponded to those of the rainbow. The ceremonial event which took place annually on this shrine furthermore symbolized the various actions of the chief supernatural being and culture hero Sun who taught the people the ceremony as it was performed by the inhabitants of the sky in the rainbow during the mythical period. Like the symbolism of many primitive peoples in America that of the Yuchi was closely connected with religious life.

It is observable that most of the geometrical figures used here as design elements, such as rectangles, triangles and zigzag lines, are commonly found in a similar capacity in other regions with, however, different and arbitrary symbolisms and interpretations in different localities. This seems to be in accord with what Dr. Boas has shown for parts of North America, that certain figures have become disseminated through wide areas and have received secondary, oftentimes symbolical, interpretations when adopted by different tribes according to their particular interests. Below, in Fig. 31, is given a summary of Yuchi conventional figures from the material at hand to facilitate the comparison of American motives and their interpretations. The significance of the various colors has already been given. To conclude this very brief account of art and symbolism a few examples of pictorial representations are given. These drawings in color were brought in by Indians to further explain various features of ethnology while investigation was being carried on. No claim is made regarding their spontaneity or native originality. In Plate IX, Fig. 10 represents a buffalo fish which has been shot with an arrow, Fig. 9 shows a cow's head with an arrow crosswise in its mouth. The picture of a mortar, pestle and two pot stirrers (Fig. 11) was drawn to show the miniature domestic utensils which are hidden away with the navel cord of a female child to influence its future. Fig. 6 represents a war club of an ancient type no longer seen, with a string of feathers. Fig. 7

Fig. 31.

1, 2 Snake.	8, 9 Morning or Evening Sky.	17-19 Stars.
3, 4 Centipede.	10 Milky Way.	20-22 Moon or Sun.
5, 6 River.	11-15 Clouds.	23-25 Sun.
7 Rainbow.	16 Sunset or Sunrise.	26, 27 Mountains.

is the sun and moon or moon and star symbol, which was placed over the entrance of the Yuchi house as a tribal mark symbolizing the kinship of the people to the sun. Fig. 8 is a design taken from a drum head. It represents the color symbolism of the cardinal points, lacking, however, the black for west. The Yuchi seem to perceive no intrinsic difference between approximate shades of green and blue. When these colors are placed side by side, however, they note an existing difference when attention is called to it. The language has one word for the two colors, *hits$_A$ⁿ'*. Shades and tones of other colors are seldom distinguished. Even the extremes do not call forth particular mention unless they border on each other. Thus indigo might be called black. Yellow and green, however, are clearly distinguished apart and are covered by particular words, *dī* yellow, *hits$_A$ⁿ'* green or blue. Aesthetically green or blue and yellow were claimed as the favorite colors by the majority of those who were questioned about the matter. It may also be noted here that designs representing cloud effects and celestial phenomena are held in the greatest fondness by the Yuchi, in which preference they may have been influenced by religious associations. The favorite patterns are commonly called by such names as *eⁿgedjinéⁿ*, 'dressed up,' and *gatsē'pongané*, 'pretty.'

Several more complex pictures are reproduced on Plate IX, which may be of native origin. They were made by a chief of his own accord on paper to illustrate several things that were mentioned in the myths. They are comparable to some of the pictures made by the plains tribes for similar purposes. Fig. 3 depicts the milky way, *tsené yuctäⁿ'*, 'dog's trail,' at night and the clear sky studded with stars. This is to explain the belief that the milky way is the trail of White Dog, a supernatural being, who travels over it every night. The ramification to the right, which is rather difficult to distinguish in the milky way, is supposed to be a blind trail leading toward the earth. The White Dog frequently blunders and takes the blind trail, getting quite near to the earth before he discovers his mistake. The Indian dogs are quick to perceive this and thereupon set up a howl which they keep up until White Dog has passed on. Thus the weird howling at night of the Indian dogs is accounted for. Fig. 2 shows the rainbow, *yū^ɛä'*, 'big house (?),' the trail over which the soul travels toward the spirit land. The brown area represents earth with a mountain in darker shade; the blue is water in the background, with sky in green above all. In Fig. 1 is a river, land, a mountain range and sky in their respective conventional colors. In the foreground are trees, and a raccoon which has been fishing and is now bound for the tree on the left where he has his hole. Fig. 5 is given to show a design used on the side pouches and shoulder straps which support them. The upper figure is a turtle, *täb^ɛä'*. The turtle and snake designs on these pouches have already been described so it is not necessary to explain their significance again. The other figures on the lower part of the

pouch are a hand and a tomahawk.   I could not find out what idea they are
intended to convey, or what their reason was for being here.   The aesthetic
and symbolic forms exhibited in pipes (Fig. 11) and clay figures (Fig.12) have
been described before and hardly need to be more than mentioned.

MUSIC.

Singing at ceremonies and dances was accompanied by drums and rattles of two kinds.

The large drum was made of hide stretched over a log sometimes three feet high and was used to call the townspeople together, and to accompany dancing. This in later times was replaced by a smaller type of drum, the pot-drum, *dĭdané* (Fig. 32) now used at ceremonies. It was made by stretching a piece of hide over an earthen pot standing about 18 inches high, containing water. An ordinary stick was used with it as a drum stick. The hide covering was decorated usually with a painted wheel-like design, suggesting a correspondence with the cardinal symbolism (See Fig. 8, Plate IX). The black for west seems to be lacking and yellow is substituted for white in this specimen. The drum had its special resting place in front of the chief's lodge in the town square and the privilege of beating it was vested in a certain individual.

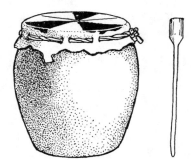

Fig. 32.   Pot Drum.

The hand rattle, *tä*ⁿ*bäné* (Pl. VII, Figs. 3, 4), was formerly a gourd, but nowadays is a cocoanut shell scraped thin and filled with small white pebbles a stick being run through the nut to serve as a handle. Small circular orifices are made in the shell to let the sound out. The gourd rattle was held at right angle to the forearm in the right hand. Sun symbols (Figure 31, Nos. 23, 25), often are carved or etched around the perforations on the shell.

A characteristic and peculiar instrument is the *tsontä′* (Pl. VII, Figs. 10, 11) the rattles worn only by women in the dances. They are composed of six to ten terrapin shells containing small white pebbles, attached to sheets of hide. Each shell has a number of holes in it and is comparable in function to the single hand rattle. One such bunch of rattles is bound to each leg below the knee. A shuffling up and down step produces a very resonant sound from this instrument. Two women usually carry them and may enter most of the dances when they have been well started. The *tsontä'* is said to be chiefly destined for the Turtle Dance, but was observed in use in others.

All of the above instruments were functionally ceremonial. There is another, however, which is strictly informal in its use. This is the flute or perhaps more properly the flageolet, *lokᴀⁿ'*, (Pl. VII, Fig. 2). It is made of cedar wood, being about two feet long and one inch in diameter. A stick of the proper thickness is split down the center and the sections gouged out until about one-eighth of an inch thick. The concave sections are then placed together in their original position and bound in five or six places with buckskin or cord. The mouthpiece is formed by simply tapering off the end abruptly. The red cedar wood used is sacred. There are six hole stops on the upper side of the lower half of the instrument. A flat piece of lead is bound with its edge at the air vent which is about four inches from the mouthpiece. The air channel to the lead is formed by the raised interior and is covered by a peculiar block of wood which is gummed and bound on. The following seven tones are produced. The pitch is about one-half a tone higher than that of the medium absolute scale.

This type of flute is one that is found widely distributed over the continent. Here as elsewhere it is employed by men as an important aid in influencing the emotions of the opposite sex. Very plaintive and touching strains are produced on the flute. They seem to have a deep effect upon the Indians, often moving the hearers to tears. Young men intentionally play these sad tunes to arouse the emotions of young girls, and the players themselves appear to be as much affected as anyone. The owner of a flute keeps his instrument wrapped up in a package and treats it with extreme care. It was formerly put to another use sometimes. When the people were traveling from a distance toward the town square to attend ceremonies there, the flute was often made to give forth a few measures of music as a sort of travelling song. When passing isolated farms or settlements on the route the flute was also played to signal the presence of the travellers and to call the hearers to join them on their journey to the town square.

One of the tunes played on the flute as a love song was recorded on the phonograph and a transcription of it is offered below. The man who gave this tune exclaimed something like the following when he had finished: "Oh, if some girls were only here! When they hear that they cry and then you can fondle them. It makes them feel lonesome. I wish some were here now. I feel badly myself."

The strain is as follows:—

The above theme is repeated over and over again with all possible variations, as shown in the five typical staffs given.

The vocal ceremonial music of the Yuchi shows one feature at least which is
rather more complex than what is generally found among Indians. The character of the music of the other southeastern tribes also resembles theirs in this
respect. The characteristic trait is that, in many of the ceremonial dance songs,
the leader gives one measure and his followers respond in chorus in another
measure or in a variation of the leader's. It resembles what is commonly
known as "round" singing where there are two members. A concrete example
will, perhaps, better illustrate this point. In one of the favorite dances, the
leader steps out from the lodge on the town square where his rank entitles him
to sit, and walks over to the fire in the center of the square, passing around it
several turns from right to left. At about the second turn he assumes a
posture and rhythmic step, holds up his elbows and sings with a deep resonant
voice

hŏ hŏ - ŏ

Before he has finished the final glide the other men, who have by this time filed
in behind him, repeat the syllables on a lower note somewhere near the end of the
glide, but with less of a musical tone

hŏ hŏ-ŏ

Immediately following this the leader repeats his first notes, changing the syllables to *hā hā—hā*. The file responds in chorus as before, changing their syllables to correspond with those of the leader. This may be repeated over again, by the leader, three or four times, sometimes varied with the syllables *hē hē—ē*, then he introduces a change.

He sings

ah! hī yo

the dancers respond with

ah! hī yo

and this is repeated four times. Then the leader changes again. With increasing vehemence he sings

ah hī yaᵉ ä

to which the dancers respond with

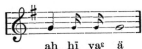

ah hī yaᵉ ä

and this is gone through four times. The leader then gives a shorter measure,

hō hō

which the other dancers repeat, sounding their first note immediately after his last. The leader now, on his part, follows without a pause with

hō hō

which the other dancers repeat after him. What has already been sung may constitute, with of course many fourfold repetitions, the first song of the dance and the leader closes it with a shrill yell which his followers echo. This type of song is very characteristic and common. There are, however, other ways of varying the "rounds," either by repeating the last two syllables of the leader's part on the same notes that he uses, or on different notes in harmony with them. Another variation has been noted in which the syllables of the line dancers' responses are entirely different from the leader's. We have, for instance, in another song

ah hī yaᵉ ä

sung by the leader, to which the dancers respond with

yō hō

and the leader finishes the couplet with

ah hī yaᵉ ä

to which the dancers answer

yō hō

Other examples of the syllables which appear in the leader's strain and in the dancers' responses can be seen in some of the dance songs which will be given later on.

It is characteristic of the ceremonial dance songs that they consist almost entirely of meaningless syllables. Only in rare instances do words appear for a few measures, to be lost again in the rhythmic jumble of mere syllabic sounds.

The rhythm of the songs which coincides in most dances with the beat of the drum or the shake of the rattle is predominantly one-two. The shuffling step of the dancers also accommodates itself to this time. The only other drum rhythms heard were three-fourths, four-fourths and an attempted tremolo which occurs oftentimes at the end of a song or where a break is made. Both of the rattles, the hand rattle and the woman's terrapin shell leg rattles, are shaken in accordance with two-fourths time, either slowly or rapidly according to the circumstances. Vehemence or excitement naturally tends to increase the speed of the rhythm.

As regards the intrinsic harmony of the dance songs it must be added that to the ordinary European ear they are remarkably agreeable. The simple rhythm accented by the drum or rattle, and visualized by the steps and motions of the dancers has a noticeable carrying force. To the natural voices of the Indians the songs in both tone and syllable, are well adapted.

Much practice in singing the dance songs from early youth makes the unison and promptness of the responses almost mechanical.

There is another feature of the dance songs deserving of mention here. It is a common thing for men who are clever in this line to compose new songs, and words to go with them. They usually choose some occasion when dancing is going on to present their pieces. Naturally, of course, there is nothing radically original in either the wording or the music of the new dance songs. They are, as far as observation goes, largely plagiarized from more or less stereotyped native sources. In presenting a new piece the composer usually steps into the dancing space between dances and leads off with some familiar introduction until a few dancers have joined in behind him. Then when all are well started he begins his composition, while those behind him simply keep on with what they commenced. So the composer as dance leader carries on his new song much to the enjoyment of his consorts and the amusement of the spectators. No drumming accompanies these dances. Unfortunately full examples of this kind of musical innovation are not available in Yuchi. Such songs do not seem to have any religious bearing whatever. Their most prominent characteristics appear to be the humorous, the obscene and, in some respects, the clownish. Part of one song composition, which I remember, describes a man's attempt to plow with a castrated hog and a bison bull harnessed together. Before the first furrow is finished, as the song goes, the hog wants to wallow in the mud and the bison bull wants a drink. Then they break out of bounds and run away, leaving the man dumbfounded. An example of obscene composition is one which alternates stanzas of meaningless syllables, such as *ya lē ha'*, *yo ha hē'*, with short phrases describing cohabitation or mentioning the private parts.[1]

The Indians regard a good singer and dancer as an accomplished man, hence no little pride is manifested in the art. Love songs are also common and are sung to give vent to related emotions, such as loneliness, sorrow, joy and other passions. One of these songs, which are, for the most part, also burdens without meaning, was given in a paper on the Creek Indians[2], but this might be taken for a Yuchi song as well, being apparently common to both tribes.

---

[1] The words of another pantomimic song of the same sort in Creek have been given in "The Creek Indians of Taskigi Town." Memoirs American Anthropological Association, Vol. II, part II, p. 138.

[2] Ibid., p. 120.

DIVISION OF TIME.

The seasons are four in number. Spring, called *hīnᴀⁿwadelé*, 'when summer is near,' is the time when agricultural activities are resumed after the comparative idleness of the winter. 'Summer,' *wädē'*, a term apparently related to *wäfá*, 'south,' is the long and active season. Autumn, *yacadīlé*, 'when the tree leaves are yellow,' is a period of combined rest, hunting and enjoyment. Winter was called *wīctá*, 'snow comes (?).' This season the people spent in idleness and recreation.

The year is further divided into moons or months, each of which has its name. The names of eleven of these moons with translations and the corresponding months in our calendar are as follows:

Sᵉ ä ɫatcpī'	Ground frozen month	January.
Ho'da dzó	Wind month	February.
Wädᵉá' sīnéⁿ	Little summer	March.
Wädᵉäᵉä'	Big summer	April.
Decᵉō' nendzó	Mulberry ripening month	May.
Cpáco nendzó	Blackberry ripening month	June.
Wagᵉä' kyä	Middle of summer	July.
Tséne agá	Dog day	August.
Tsogá lī'ne tseᵉe	Hay cutting month	September.
Tsotᵉō' hoⁿstäné	Corn ripening month	October.
Ho'ctᴀⁿdᵉä' kyä	Middle of winter	December.

The passage of time during the day time is commonly observed by glancing at the sun. During the night time the moon and stars, if the weather is clear, serve the same purpose.

The day itself is divided into different periods equivalent, in our reckoning, to morning, noon, afternoon and evening. The names for these are *ägyälé*, 'at dawn,' 'morning'; *yūbaɫéⁿ*, 'noon,' derivative from *yū'ba* 'high,' referring to the sun; *padonᴀⁿhogyé*, 'afternoon,' 'toward the night;' *fᵉā* 'evening,' and lastly, *pado'* 'night.'

SOCIAL AND POLITICAL ORGANIZATION.

The social and political organization of the Yuchi is, for a primitive people, rather complex. What is offered here upon this subject probably does not represent all that could be said; neither is it to be supposed that the Indians of today retain a complete knowledge of earlier social conditions.

The social groups outside of the ordinary family consisting of man, wife or wives and offspring, are two, namely the clan, and another which for want of better terms we may call the society or class. The whole tribal community, inclusive of the various groups, forms another unit with special institutions, called the town. At several periods in history the town has been co-terminous with the tribe. At other times, when its settlements have been scattered over wider areas, the tribe has divided itself into several towns, some of these assuming independent names and the privileges of self control in political and religious matters. Anticipating somewhat the discussion of the clans we find these to be maternal totemic groups with the regulation of exogamy. These clans number about twenty. The society or class divisions, on the other hand, show a grouping of the males of the tribe into a two-fold division. This identity descends from father to son, certain public offices connected with religious ceremonies and political matters going with it. The societies, besides, are the only social divisions which have distinctive personal insignia, in the form of designs in facial painting. Lastly the town, or the tribe, we shall find to be the all-embracing institution with its elective officials, its annual religious ceremonials and its public square-ground where councils and social gatherings are held, and which, once a year, becomes, in the native mind, a religious shrine where the whole community is expected to assemble for the annual ceremonies.

After the Yuchi became a part of the confederacy instituted by the Creek (Muskogi) tribes a slight development is to be noted. The tribe then became politically a town of the confederacy and had to appoint a representative to the confederacy council, without, however, suffering the loss of its independence in most matters. The Yuchi tribe thereafter owed a certain amount of support to the Creek confederacy and was to a slight extent subject to its military decisions.

KINSHIP.

The family, in our sense of the word, as a group is of very little social or political importance in the tribe. The father has a certain individual social standing according to his clan and according to his society. The woman on the other hand carries the identity of the children, who may be said to belong to her. The bonds of closest kinship, however, being reckoned chiefly through the mother, it would appear that the closest degrees of consanguinity are counted in the clan. This matter of kinship is better illustrated by the list of terms which I give below. The list does not claim to be exhaustive.

1. *dītso t^{ε}ä$^{n\prime}$*, my father.
2. *dītso hä$^{n\prime}$*, my mother.
3. *dī s^{ε}äné*,   my son.
4. *dī^{ε}yäné*, my daughter.
5. *dī go^{ε}né*, my child (indefinite).
6. *dītso dané*, my brother, my clan brother.
7. *dītso wa^{ε}né*, my sister, my mother's sister's daughter.
8. *dītso djīné*, my children (both sexes), great grandchildren, etc.
9. *dītso hä^{n}sī′* (literally "my little mother") my mother's sister.
10. *dītso t^{ε}ä^{n}sī′*, (literally "my little father") my mother's brother, my father's brother.
11. *dī^{ε}yʌ$^{n\prime}$*, my mother's sister's son.
12. *dī lahá*, my father's sister, my mother's mother, my mother's grandmother, great-grandmother, etc., my father's mother (and her sisters and brothers).
13. *dītso^{3}ō′*, my mother's father, my mother's grandfather, great-grandfather, etc., my father's father (and his sisters and brothers).
14. *dī ga'tʌ$^{n\prime}$*, my wife, (if there is more than one all are included under the same term), my husband (woman speaking).
15. *dītso géwosahʌ$^{n\prime}$*, my wife's father, my wife's mother.
16. *dītso kyäné*, my wife's sister, my wife's father's sister, my wife's mother's sister.
17. *dītso djäné*, my wife's brother, my wife's father's brother, my wife's mother's brother.
18. *dī ga'tī′*, my friend.

A few remarks on this list will perhaps make the reckoning somewhat clearer. The children of the father's sisters and the children of the brother are not in the list, as they are expressed, not by any specific term of relationship, but by a combination of the involved terms, i. e., *dī lahá se s^{ε}äné*, 'my father's sister, her son', and *dītso dané ho^{n}s^{ε}äné*, 'my brother, his son.'

So also with the children of 'my wife's brothers and sisters,' and 'my wife's father's sisters and brothers.' In fact, by means of the first six terms (omitting

5) almost any relationship can be expressed. It is, moreover, frequently done in this way by those who are not well informed on the terms.[1]

The terms of relationship from 14 onwards answer as well for a man speaking as for a woman speaking.

It can readily be seen from this list that the lines of closest kinship are within the clan. (See 6, 7, 9, 10, 11.)

Contrary to what might be expected in America, it appears that no distinction in terms is made between elder or younger brothers and sister· and elder or younger sons and daughters.

Sex appears to be a distinctive characterizer as shown in most of the equivalents for *dī lahá* (12) and *dīts³o ō'* (13).

It is also rather peculiar that, after the first generation from the speaker, posterity is not differentiated, but is grouped promiscuously under the one term *dītso djīné* (8).

The Clans.

One of the social units of the Yuchi requiring to be taken up in detail is the clan. This is a group in which membership is reckoned through maternal descent. The members of each clan believe that they are the relatives and, in some vague way, the descendants of certain pre-existing animals whose names and identity they now bear. The animal ancestors are accordingly totemic. In regard to the living animals, they, too, are the earthly types and descendants of the pre-existing ones, hence, since they trace their descent from the same sources as the human clans, the two are consanguinely related.

This brings the various clan groups into close relationship with various species of animals and we find accordingly that the members of each clan will not do violence to wild animals having the form and name of their totem. For instance, the Bear clan people never molest bears, but nevertheless they use commodities made from parts of the bear. Such things, of course, as bear hides, bear meat or whatever else may be useful, are obtained from other clans who have no taboo against killing bears. In the same way the Deer people use parts of the deer when they have occasion to, but do not directly take part in killing deer.

In this way a sort of amnesty is maintained between the different clans and different kinds of animals while the blame for the injury of animals is shifted from one clan to the other. General use could consequently be made of the animal kingdom without obliging members of any clan to be the direct murderers of their animal relatives.

---

[1] To illustrate this I might add that several times young men who were asked for various terms of relationship gave the indirect or combined expressions instead of the actual term. For instance, I was given *ditso hän' hon gáwa⁸né*, 'my mother. her sister,' instead of *ditso hänsi'*, "my little mother,' 'my mother's sister' (9).

In common usage the clan is known collectively by its animal name: the men of the Panther clan calling themselves Panthers, those of the Fish clan, Fish, and so on through the list. The totemic animals are held in reverence, appealed to privately in various exigencies, and publicly worshipped in dances during the annual ceremony so often referred to.

The idea of the clan or totem is expressed by the word *yū'ta*, 'on the house.' The Bear clan, for instance, is designated by the expression *sag^ē'* *yūta*, 'bear on the house,' or, in a somewhat different manner, by the expression *sag^ē'taha*, 'those who have the bear on them.' By these etymologies, the inference is that in former times, the members of one clan resided together in the same dwelling under the same totem, and that some realistic or symbolic sign about the person distinguished the different clansfolk from each other. It should be recalled in this connection that the tribal totem, the sun, was painted over the doorway of the Yuchi house and that the men wore decorative designs in beadwork which indicated their affinity to the sun. Clan totemic designs may have been displayed in a like manner.

It will be shown later on that the young man or boy in the course of his adolescence reaches a period when he is initiated into the rank of manhood in his town. This event is connected with totemism. For from the time of his initiation he is believed to have acquired the protection of his clan totem. Thenceforth he stands in a totemic relation similar to the young man of the plains tribes who has obtained his "medicine." Here in the Southeast, however, the "medicine" is not represented by a concrete object, but is the guiding influence of a supernatural being. The earthly animals nevertheless are believed in many cases to possess wisdom which may be useful to human beings, so the different clans look to their animal relatives for aid in various directions. Among the tribes of the plains, however, each man has an individual guardian spirit, which is not necessarily the same as his gens totem.

From several informants the following list of clans has been collected, but there seems to be some doubt about those which are marked * as they were not generally agreed upon.

1	Bear, *Sag^ē'*.	11	Otter, *Cūłané*.
2	Wolf, *Dałá*.	12	Raccoon, *Djä'tīe^n*.
3	Deer, *We^ɛyA^n'*.	13	Skunk, *YūsA^n'*.
4	Tortoise, *Täb^ɛä'*.	14	Opossum, *WētsagowA^n'*.
5	Panther, *Wētc^ɛA^n'*.	15	Rabbit, *Cadjwané*.
6	Wildcat, *Cad^ɛané*.	16	Squirrel, *Cáya*.
7	Fox, *Catiené*.	17	Turkey, *Wētc^ɛá*.
8	Wind, *Godá*.	18	Eagle*, *Câ'na*.
9	Fish, *Cū*.	19	Buzzard*, *YA^ntī'*.
10	Beaver, *Cagä^n'*.	20	Snake*, *Ca*.

A mythical origin is ascribed to clans.   When the earth was completed, the beings upon it were made to assemble and told to advance to a certain distance.   Upon their return, in full view of the assembly, some would ask, "What does he look like?"   Then *Gohä'ntonē'*, a supernatural being, gave them names according to the nature that they exhibited in their movements.   Those who jumped on trees became birds, and those showing other physical peculiarities became various animals, thenceforth the ancestors of clans.   This account, taken from the Creek, is asserted by the Indians to be identical with that of the Yuchi.   Tribal myths relating to the various exploits of animals that appear in the clan list are told for the purpose of praising the totem and showing his superiority over the other totems.   Into this class some negro myth elements, and perhaps whole animal tales, may have become incorporated, since each clan welcomes praiseworthy stories of its totem's exploits and is ready to repeat such tales as though they were of native origin.   Most Indians, however, distinguish between what is original and what is borrowed.

The social rank of these clans is not equal throughout.   Four at least are classed above the others, and from one of them the town chief is chosen.   Others, given at the foot of the list are rather looked down upon and seldom if ever represented in official positions.

The town chief of the Yuchi, the four head chiefs of the ceremonies, and the medicine priest, must be chosen from either the Bear, Wolf, Tortoise or Deer clans.   There is some attempt made to have two of the four ceremonial chiefs from two different clans.   At the last celebration of the ceremonies two were from the Bear clan and two from the Wolf, the town chief himself being a Bear.   The neighboring Creek towns are likewise headed by a member of the leading clan in each town.   The modern explanation given for this hegemony is that the head clan is the most numerous and most powerful in the town, but the real explanation, as in all such cases, is probably a very different one, although we have no means of knowing what it is.   The next to the highest official at the ceremonies, the *goconé*, who represents the Warrior society, is usually taken from the Panther clan.

No particular insignia is found to distinguish the different clans from one another.   There are, furthermore, no esoteric clan ceremonies among the Yuchi, all clan religious worship being held in common by the town at the annual festival.   Dances are likewise performed by the townsmen irrespective of their clan, the dances being for the honor and propitiation of the clan totem for whom the dance is named.   It would appear from this that the clan organizations and clan religious rites have become subordinated to the town organization in the course of time.   Direct historical evidence for such a supposition, however, is wanting, except for the fact that in their old home the Yuchi are reported to have lived in clan communities more centralized than we find them now.

No clan groups or phratries are recognized at the present time, nor are clans subdivided. There are, besides, no historical evidences of convergence. From the beginning clans are believed to have remained separate and distinct and must continue so.   In regard to the antiquity of the present clan system it appears that no historical changes have taken place, except where occasional extinction may have occurred.

One fact should, however, be mentioned, at least in connection with a possible clan grouping in some former period. Reference is made, in a myth to a time when the tribe was holding a dance. The people were divided into two bands, those dancing with bear hides over the shoulders and known as the Bear-hide people, *sagᵉ ē hʌntcwá,* and those dancing with wildcat skins, the Wildcat-hide people, *cätīenē' hʌntcwá.* A dispute arose amongst them and the two groups separated. The Bear-hide people departed westward and were never heard from again. Those that remain today are all Wildcat people. What the historical significance of this myth or tradition may be it is unsafe to say. The important restriction of exogamy which holds for all the clans equally, will be described under marriage.

Until recently the blood-feud prevailed, but reprieve was granted to an offender who was able to get inside the public-square ground during the annual ceremonies without being apprehended. Maintenance of clan honor and reverence for their totem were exacted of all people, because the displeasure of the totem was feared. As the taboo of taking the life or eating the flesh of the totemic animal rested upon all, should the taboo be broken, propitiation had to be made in the nature of a fine, which was paid to the clan, either in live stock or property, else the offender was punished by a whipping.

Upon the death of a man the ordinary property of the household which properly belonged to him is divided among his own and his sister's children who are naturally of his clan. All of the personal property of a woman descends to her children. If she has none, it goes to her nearest clan relatives.

CRIMES AND PUNISHMENTS.

Before becoming subject to our laws the Yuchi had their own regulations in regard to crime. Punishments were not inflicted by any organized body, but it was understood that whoever discovered the wrong, or whoever caught the wrongdoer, had the privilege of giving the punishment. The clan as a body was often the agent.

Murder was considered the greatest wrong. The clan of the victim usually hunted down the culprit and took vengeance upon him. Sometimes, however, only the immediate family was concerned. When the murderer was found he was killed as nearly as possible in the same way that he had committed the murder. If the murderer had used a knife on the victim, then he was executed with a knife, the same one if possible. If he had used a rifle then he was shot in the same way that he had done the deed. No vengeance, however, was undertaken by the clan of a murderer for his death. There was only one way for a man who was outlawed for a misdemeanor to be forgiven, and that was for him to hide away until the next harvest ceremony and then try to get safely inside the town square during the event. If he succeeded in this he was not molested and was thereafter exempt from vengeance.

Adultery and fornication were the next most serious offences. The husband or his family were the agents of punishment in this case, although anyone discovering the parties in the act had the right to inflict mutilation. Fornicators and adulterers when caught were invariably punished by having their ears cut off. The man and the woman were both treated in this way.

Thieving was a minor offence and the matter was usually settled without much of a disturbance, the property being returned or an equivalent rendered.

Personal injury was revenged by personal retaliation. Sometimes, however, the victim's clan would help him to retaliate.

It would also happen that sometimes families, or a few townspeople, would band together to rid the community of an undesirable member, or to inflict chastisement on some intolerable mischief maker. For instance, it often happened that young women who were pestered too much by some man would conspire together, waylay him and abuse him until they thought he had enough of a lesson. Not infrequently men of this sort were very seriously mutilated by enraged and vindictive women. A case is remembered where a woman cut off the private parts of a man who had forced her into cohabitation.

THE SOCIETIES.

Another social grouping entirely separate and distinct from the clan system exists among the Yuchi. Its members are not necessarily considered as kin, but represent two divisions of the tribe which include the entire male population. Every male child is born into one of these two divisions and counts his eligibility to membership through his father. The two divisions are the Chief society and the Warrior society, respectively, *balé^n* and *sä^{n}bá*. Inherited membership in these societies is as rigid as it is in the clan, alienation being impossible. Certain rights belong to these societies, which will be described in separate paragraphs. But perhaps the chief idea concerned with them is that the Chief society is a peace band, and the Warrior society is a war band. Tribal subdivisions based on the same functional idea are characteristic of several other southern tribes, among whom may be mentioned the Creeks, and the Osage. Undoubtedly, when more is known, other tribes will be found to have similar institutions. The Sauk, for instance, have something apparently quite similar.[1]

---

[1] As so little on the subject of the social subdivisions among the southern and southeastern tribes has appeared in print, it seems advisable to present here what little is available for comparison.

The Creek tribes in general recognized the difference in function between two classes of men in some of which membership was elective. These were the Chiefs and the Warriors, the former less numerous but more influential in some towns, the latter having the political control in other towns In Taskigi town, for example, the highest permanent authority was a Chief instead of a Warrior, on account of which the town was classed as a white or peace town. Facial painting among the Taskigi had for its object the designation of the two divisions. (Cf. Creek Indians of Taskigi town, pp. 111, 114.)

Among the Chickasaw all the clans are grouped into two divisions which, in sentiment, are manifestly ill-disposed to each other, reciprocally attributing sickness to each other, holding separate ceremonies, having separate officers, a separate camping place, and wearing different facial painting. Here, too, one group is held in higher esteem, the other being considered inferior. (Cf. Notes on Chickasaw Ethnology, Journal American Folk-Lore, Vol. XX, p. 51).

The Osage gentes are grouped together in two divisions, politically opposite in function. The one is for war, the other for peace, each having its own camping place, personal marks, officers and local interests. (Cf. Siouan Sociology, Fifteenth Report Bureau American Ethnology, 1893-94, and Notes on the Ethnology of the Osage Indians, Transactions of the Department of Archeology, University of Pennsylvania, Vol. II, part 2, p. 166-7).

"The warriors of the Saukie nation are divided into two bands or parties, one of which is called Kishkoquis, or the 'Long Hairs,' and the other Oshkush, the brave...... The Kishkoquis, or 'Long Hairs,' are commanded by the hereditary war chief Keokuk, whose standard is red; the head man of the Oshkushies is Kaipolequa......whose standard is blue. The 'Long Hairs' take precedence in point of rank. The formation of these parties is a matter of national concern, and is effected by a simple arrangement. The first male child who is born to a Kishkoquis is marked with white paint, the distinguishing color of the Kishkoquis, and belongs to that party; the next male of the same family is marked with black paint, and is attached to the Oshkushies, and so on alternately, the first son belonging to the band with his father, and the others being assigned in turn first to one band, and then to the other. Thus all the warriors are attached to one or the other band, and the division is as nearly equal as it could be by any arrangement commencing with infancy.

"Whenever the whole nation or any large party of warriors turns out to engage in a grand hunt, or a warlike expedition, or for the purpose of performing sham battles, or ball plays, the individuals belonging to the two bands are distinguished by their appropriate colors. If the purpose of the assemblage is for sham fighting, or other diversion, the Kishkoquis daub their bodies all over with white clay, and the Oshkushies blacken themselves with charcoal; the bands are ranged under their respective leaders and play against each other rallying under the red and blue banners. In war and in hunting, when all must be ranged on one side, the white and the black paints are mingled with other colors, so that the distinction is kept up, and after the close of the expedition......the trophies of each band collectively are compared and the deeds of each repeated. The object of these societies will be readily seen. They form a part of the simple machinery of a military government... From early youth each individual is taught to feel that ....the honor of his band as well as his own is concerned in his success or failure............."

Cf. McKenny and Hall, History of the Indian Tribes of North America, etc., Philadelphia, 1848, vol. I, p. 117.

The Chief society, *balén*, has the right of being seated, during ceremonies, in the west lodge of the town square, and from its ranks are chosen the highest public officials. Four chiefs occupy the front of the lodge, the principal or town chief being of their number and their head. These four are the first to come forward to participate in the ceremonial events. In the town council it is a Chief who must light the pipe and start it around. The main recognized function of the Chief society is to manage the governmental affairs of the town so that peace is preserved. They are, above all, conservative in everything. If anything, the Chiefs hold themselves above the Warriors in general esteem. They are the thinkers, the speakers, the dignified superiors of the town.

Although there exists no strictly regular design for the facial decoration of a Chief, yet the following limitations are traditionally observed. Little or no black is used, both eyes are surrounded with red, and usually on each cheek alternating bars, less than two inches long, of blue and yellow are laid horizontally (Pl. X, Fig. 5). Frequently three small blue spots are placed in a line between the corner of the eye and the temple (Fig. 8). Any of these markings may be omitted or varied to suit personal fancy, yet the characteristics are prominently retained. The young child members of the Chief society, who have not yet been formally initiated to the band, are usually decorated with red on the eyebrows, cheeks and forehead (Fig. 2). It is asserted that this society has the privilege of exercising more freedom in the use of various colors than the Warrior society.

The Warrior society, *säⁿbá*, has four representatives, who are seated two in the north lodge and two in the south lodge, during the ceremonies. One of their number is head, and is called *goconé*. He is the highest in rank of the Warrior society his special office during the ceremonies being to insure continuous dancing, to take care of the fire while dancing is going on, and to appoint players in the ball game. The Warrior society forms one side in the ball game; they are known as mean players, while their opponents, being of the other society, display a more dignified demeanor. The four Warriors are second to the Chiefs and follow them when the emetic is taken. This society also supplies the official who performs the scratching operation at the ceremonies. In the council and at the ceremonies the common members of the Warrior society are seated in the north and south lodges, ranged behind their representatives. Their tendency in political affairs was formerly, to advocate the appeal to arms. When war was decided upon, the Warriors embarked in a body under their head man, who might accordingly be called a sort of war chief.

The characteristic pattern of this society is to have one half of the face red, the other black, (Pl. X, Fig. 7). A variation of this pattern, said to be a simplification, is to paint only one eye socket black and the other red. Accompanying this modification the upper lip is often blackened (Fig. 3).

Exceptions to the above formulæ in facial decoration are quite frequent and unexplainable.   At the 1905 ceremonies one occupant of the Warrior lodge had merely a red line drawn from the corners of the mouth to the angle of the jaw bone (Pl. X, Fig. 1). Both in 1904 and 1905 the Yuchi town chief wore no paint whatever, neither did the functionary who performed the scratching operation. Chiefs have been observed at other times with red blotches or two or three red bars on the cheeks (Fig. 6).

If anything, something of a hostile feeling is manifested and felt between the two societies. This is allowed to break out in a mild way, upon the occasion of the ball game, where, as before stated, the two societies make up opposite sides. Jealousy on the part of the Warriors may be at the bottom of this. The inheritance of property partially follows the paternal line, thereby keeping within each society much of the property of its members. At his death each male among the Yuchi is painted with the design appropriate to his society, and slight differences in mortuary observances are supposed to exist. A mythical origin is ascribed to the societies. A supernatural being, Gohäntoné, is believed to have been their originator, as was stated by those who claimed to know anything at all on the subject.

In general, it may be added that at the annual ceremony the office of the Chief society is to care for the medicine plants and their administration, while the Warrior society presides over dancing and games, each society being represented in the field of ceremonial action by the four members with special privileges. In all affairs, however, the Chief society takes precedence.

From all appearances men of the Chief class prefer to have their daughters marry Chiefs rather than Warriors for the sake of maintaining the social superiority of their line. There is, though, no strict rule about this. If the tendency toward endogamy were carried much further in the societies, they might be described as non-totemic gentes, in the restricted American sense of the term, and we should have an instance here of both a clan and a gentile system flourishing in the same tribe.

When the whole matter is considered as it stands among the Yuchi today, it seems, if anything, that the society organization has a more prominent place in the social life of the town than the clan organization. Whereas the position of town chief is kept in the hands of a certain clan and many of the ceremonial dances are supposed to have been formerly more in the nature of clan dances, we find, nevertheless, that military, religious and most political officers are chosen according to their society. As for military and most political matters of the town they are quite evidently more the concerns of the societies than of the clans.

As nothing definite regarding the actual history of the society organization can be stated, it can only be said that the two social groups exist side by side, having the tribal honors and privileges fairly equally divided between them.

In a general way there appear to be some points of resemblance between these divisions and the ceremonial and military societies of the plains. The simple inheritance of the society privileges, which characterizes the Southeast, offers a contrast in some respects to the custom as we find it in other regions. In some tribes of the plains heraldic and society rights invested in sacred bundles are transmitted by sale and purchase, while among the Kwakiutl, whose social organization has been thoroughly studied, and so serves well for purposes of comparison, the rights to ceremonies and heraldry are acquired by marriage.

To a certain extent, bearing in mind the feeling of superiority on the part of the Chiefs, and their position in the town, the two Yuchi society groups remind one of the social castes of the Natchez, if we rightly interpret the nature of the latter from historical records.

The Town and Town Square.

We now come to the consideration of the town. This is the ruling institution in the life of the Yuchi, the same holding true for most of the other southeastern tribes. It has superseded in political importance the other social groupings, and, as far as any governmental activities are carried on at all, they too are the affairs of the town. The societies are represented by officers in town gatherings, while some of the clans have assumed the right to fill the highest town office, as we have seen before. The town is extremely democratic, however, as all of the men are expected to be present at its meetings, having the equal right to express opinions upon public matters which may be up for debate and to acclaim their vote for or against candidates for the town offices. The ritualistic and ceremonial life of the community is also a matter of town interest. The chief religious rites take place once a year publicly in the town square. Here again every male is a common participant in the events that take place, and the leaders of the minor social groups become for the time the ceremonial officials as well. Besides these officials, with double functions as it were, there are several others who do not seem to have any special concern with clan or society, but who have to do chiefly with the town when it is assembled either on religious or political occasions.

The Yuchi town, consisting of families, clans, and societies, forms by itself an independent social group, as has been shown. The identity, politically speaking, between the terms town and tribe has also been mentioned. There are three such towns recognized today, one of them less important than the others: Polecat, Sand Creek, and Big Pond, the last being the least. The town comprises an area of settlement having a common public ceremonial and council square-ground. It has a chief representative, who is called 'bále^n,' the chief religious official as well. He was also the representative of his town in the Creek House of Kings. Two towns, Polecat and Sand Creek, perform an annual ceremony at which the presence of all townsmen is required, under penalty of a fine which is paid to the four principal chiefs and used to defray the expenses of the attendant feast.[1]

Membership in the town is decided entirely by birth. But with proper recognition a stranger who marries a Yuchi woman may become a member by being initiated at the annual ceremonies. Initiation merely consists in undergoing the ceremonial operations with the men of the town. The town has the power to make peace or war. Redress for individual wrongs inflicted by aliens is demanded by the town, and the town, furthermore, must be party to all undertakings or stipulations with foreigners.

In taking a view of the old town idea and the later developed Creek Confederacy, let us consider the condition of the Yuchi in their original seats, in the east. There they lived in scattered communities, each having a public town square and town ceremony just as today. Representatives were chosen to appear at the tribal gatherings which occurred once a year when all the settlements or villages were assembled. With the inroads of the unorganized Muskogi from the west, and their incorporation of the indigenous southeastern stocks, it would be very natural for them to seize upon a town system which was found on the soil, well fitted to their mode of life and adaptable to a loose protective confederacy. The loose confederacy then, when the Muskogi had completed their conquest of the natives and become properly organized, appeared as nothing more than an improved and extended type of the town system in vogue among themselves and the Yuchi.

THE TOWN SQUARE.—The center of the town is a square plot of ground kept free from vegetation and trampled down smooth and hard all over. This plot is known as the rainbow, or big house, *yūᵉä′*. Its four sides face north, east, south and west respectively. Here is the sacred ground of the town where civil and ceremonial events take place. The square, moreover, is the town itself in sentiment. It is located near water, and at a point convenient to the townsfolk. Its sides are about 75 feet in extent. Three lodges constructed of upright posts roofed with brush, open on all sides, stand on its borders, one on the north, one on the west and one on the south side of the square. In the center of the square is a spot where the fire is kept burning during night gatherings. Some idea of the general appearance of the town square and the lodges can be obtained from the photographs illustrating the different stages of the ceremonies (Plates XII-XIV). The architecture of the lodges is the same as that of the dwellings figured before. It is commonly reported, however, that some generations ago the lodges on the square-ground were quite different from those of today. They were

---

[1] In the 1905 ceremonies, the *goconé*, through intoxication, was unable to undergo the scratching operation. For this, he and several others were each fined $2.50 by the chiefs. If money is not forthcoming the equivalent in stock or property is exacted.

without roofs, being merely four tiers of logs intended for seats. These were graded in elevation so as to afford all the audience an unobstructed view of the square. The front and lowest seat consisted simply of a log resting

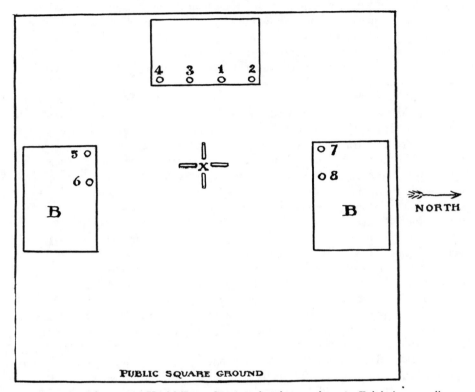

Fig. 33.   Diagram of Yuchi Town Square, showing seating of officials in council.

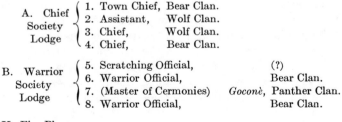

A. Chief Society Lodge	1. Town Chief,	Bear Clan.
	2. Assistant,	Wolf Clan.
	3. Chief,	Wolf Clan.
	4. Chief,	Bear Clan.

B. Warrior Society Lodge	5. Scratching Official,		(?)
	6. Warrior Official,		Bear Clan.
	7. (Master of Cermonies)	*Goconè*,	Panther Clan.
	8. Warrior Official,		Bear Clan.

X. Fire Place.

upon the ground. The second was several feet higher, supported by crotched or forked posts. The third was still higher, and the last bank of seats was some feet above the ground, enabling those sitting there to see over the heads of the spectators in front.

A diagram of the town square showing the seating arrangement for the inhabitants and for the different groups and officials is given in Fig. 33. It should be added that the ordinary members of the Chief society are ranged on log seats behind their leaders 1, 2, 3, 4 in the west lodge A. The other two lodges, B, are for the Warriors whose leaders are seated at 5, 6, 7, and 8. The clans of the various officials are given with the explanation of the figure, to show how these are represented among the leaders at the time of this writing. No particular arrangement in the location of different clans and societies about the square seems to have been thought of. Aliens and strangers are allowed on the square-ground at all times except during the second day of the annual ceremony.

Only the political aspect of the town square has been thus far dealt with. Its religious aspect, however, is even of greater importance It has already been said that the square-ground symbolizes the rainbow. In this sense it represents the rainbow as the town square of the supernatural beings, the idea having been brought to earth, with instructions to perpetuate it, by the tribal deity, the Sun. In emulation of the supernatural beings who were holding a meeting upon the rainbow in the world above when the Sun himself was born, the earthly people now congregate upon the earthly rainbow-shrine for their communal events. At the time of the annual ceremonies the square-ground is decorated in places with colored material, ashes, paint and vegetation to carry out the symbolism, the place becoming, for the time, a great religious emblem. As this, however, is more closely connected with religion than with the present heading, the description of the square as a tribal shrine is reserved for another place.

Town Officials and Council.

TOWN OFFICIALS.—The following deals with various town officials and their functions, as far could be learned. The officers are given in the list in the order of their rank.

Bále^n gabidáne.—A tribal chief having this title is chosen for life to represent the tribe in the Creek confederacy councils.

Bale^{nε}ä'.—This is a town chief elected from the Bear clan as the civil and religious head. He must be of Chief class. A worthy clansman of his is chosen to assist him and to inherit his place. This man, too, has an important place in the ceremonies and is called also *bále^n*.

Bále^n.—Three Chiefs having this title comprise the town chief's staff.

Goconé.—This is a master of ceremonies from the Panther clan and represents the highest official of the Warrior society. He is the treasurer, so to speak, of the town and possesses the power of a kind of policeman. He is the master of dances and the fire guardian at the night ceremonies. His duties cease at the beginning of the ball game which concludes the annual ceremony.

Goconé or *Säⁿbá*.—Three other Warriors comprises the staff of the preceding officer, being called also *goconé*. They, with the master-of-ceremonies, form a sort of Warrior committee.

All of these officers are both the civil and religious functionaries upon ceremonial occasions. The qualifier *yūᵋahé*, 'square ground,' is prefixed to their titles, as in *yūᵋahō'baleⁿ*.

The following few officers seem to have had occasion for employment only at the annual·ceremonies, in the various capacities mentioned.

Yätcigī'.—Four young men about to be initiated were given their first official duties under leadership of one of their number. They were the actual police of the public square, their badges of office being staffs about seven feet long. They had to keep women and dogs from the square and to prevent men from sleeping or leaning against posts during ceremonies. They handled the sacred fire materials and procured and prepared the emetic. They will be mentioned again later. This town square ceremonial service was really the culmination of their initiation period, and the young men entered into full tribal manhood after it was over.

Gondīné or *Yatsá*.—The scratcher, one of the four *goconé*, was chosen from the Warrior society to perform the ceremonial scratching operation upon the men.

Ka'ká, 'white man.'—Two butchers had entire charge of the feast preparations at the ceremony. Their insignia were also staffs. They were also the heralds for the town at this time.

All of these offices are given by simple election or appointment in council in the public square, and are held for life unless deposition is warranted on grounds of inefficiency or for some other good reason. The *yatcigī'*, however, leave their office when they marry and other boys take their places.

THE COUNCIL.—The Yuchi council is the town assembly under the charge of the officials. It is held in the public square at intervals appointed by the town chief, as a rule lasting all day. Every townsman is expected to be present and seated in either the Chief lodge or the Warrior lodges, according to his society. The four principal chiefs occupy the front log of their lodge and the four '*goconé*', two in each opposite Warrior lodge, are seated upon the front log of that lodge. The town chief is the first to speak announcing the purpose of the assembly. From the fire, which is started in the usual place in the center of the square, a pipe is lighted by a member of the Chief society and passed around. After due deliberation in smoking a speech can be made by anyone wishing to do so. It is usual, however, for the town chief to be the first to make an address. He rises from his seat and states the subject under consideration, at the same time giving words of advice and asking for serious thought in connection with the matter. Should the town chief for any reason not wish to make the speech himself, he can dictate it to an assistant, who will commit it to memory and, at the proper time, deliver it in public as though he were the town chief himself.

In times of the election of officials, speeches are made by the supporters of the candidates, or those opposing them, until a majority is reached in the case of each candidate. This is necessary in all elections to office. In the actual election or casting of ballots, the men of the town assemble on the town square in a long line. Then, as they start to walk toward the town chief, those who are in favor of the candidate step out of the line to one side. A man of the Warrior society, usually the *goconé*, counts them and reports the result to the town chief, who concludes with a speech of inauguration. Councils and elections of this sort are usually ended by night-time and the towns folk then fall to dancing in the square-ground until daybreak. The seating in the council is the same as that in the ceremonies. The decisions of the body are made public throughout the town and carried into effect by the *goconé*. Two Warriors often serve as heralds during council meetings and during the ceremonies. These are the *ka'kà*. They are a sort of police as well.

The Yuchi tribe has a head chief who is known as its highest representative. His town, the Polecat settlement, is now the center of religious and political activity.

Every individual not a Yuchi by blood is held as an inferior, and a separate pronominal gender in the language distinguishes the Yuchi from all other tribes and races. Nevertheless, men of other tribes often marry Yuchi women and thenceforth are obliged, under penalty of a fine, to take part in tribal activities. Such, however, are not often elected to offices. They sit in the Warrior society lodges in the square. A few Creeks and Shawnees are thus intermingled with the Yuchi. As a part of the Muskogi confederacy, the Yuchi tribe occupied an equal place with the various other tribes and stocks that composed this body. Officially it was called in Creek, Yuchi Town, *Yū'tsi tálwa*, and sent one representative to the Creek House of Kings and four (sometimes called Commissioners) to the House of Warriors at Muscogee, I. T., the then capital of the Creek Nation. Yuchi Town is looked upon as quite an important one in the confederacy, for it always has been somewhat aggressive.

If in conclusion we interpret the social conditions correctly it would appear, from what has been said, that certain of the clans had established their own prominence in the village community, made up different totemic groups, and assumed the prerogative of filling the highest governmental office, namely that of town chief. From this point on, we may venture to say, the various social elements of the town obtained representation in public offices until a balance of power was reached and the present town organization resulted.

WARFARE.

The military was only a moderately developed institution with the Yuchi. As far as we are able to judge, the training of young men for the war path was undertaken as a means of defense, rather than for the purpose of aggression. The original idea was apparently to maintain the political unity of the tribe, and to protect its territory against the encroachments of foreigners. The town council, consisting of the chief as chairman and representatives from the Chief and Warrior societies, together with war leaders and other old men of integrity and experience, exercised the privilege of declaring war against an enemy, calling all the able-bodied men of the Warrior class into action. In such a case the town was said to "go out" and the movement was a unanimous, tribal one. The matter, however, would be debated in the town square for some time, the Warrior society usually clamoring for action, the Chief society bringing to bear a conservative influence on the debate.

On the whole, little seems to be known of the military history of this tribe. Hawkins states that Benjamin Harrison attacked one of the Yuchi towns and killed sixteen gun men. Historically we know of another such instance during the Creek War, 1814, when the Yuchi joined the Creeks in an effort to repulse General Jackson and suffered, in consequence, quite serious losses at the hands of the troops. They as a tribe no doubt supported the Creek towns at other times after their incorporation into the Creek Confederacy.

There was, however, nothing to prevent the gratification of individual inclinations toward making up parties for raiding or for war with other tribes. The Yuchi, like typical Indians, often proceeded to do this. Such parties often comprised the members of a clan who were bent on retaliation, or they might be made up of restless, violent fellows who thirsted for excitement or plunder. In such a project, we are told, the town itself had no share of responsibility and often manifested openly its disapproval. Neither would the town acknowledge the blame before the representatives of other tribes which had been assaulted by such parties.

For warfare the Yuchi used the same kind of bows and arrows as for hunting. These have been described. In addition, a club, gēgᵉané or yäkᵉä́', was carried. A sketch of one of these is given, Pl. IX, Fig. 6, as it was remembered by an Indian. Its handle was of wood and the head was a wooden ball. A string of feathers ran from the end of the handle to the head. Axes with stone, and later with iron heads, are remembered to have been used. They were called tcīdī́'. A modification of the iron tomahawk, tcīdī́'yudᵉa', 'tomahawk pipe,' was much in vogue, during the colonial times, among the

Yuchi as among most of the eastern tribes. These, of course, were obtained from white traders. Nothing, however, is remembered of spears or shields.

Before going into action the warriors were careful to have their faces painted with the design appropriate to their society or class. A head covering or helmet was made of leather stiffened and rounded on top to deaden the impact of a club or arrow. The whole affair was rather low and dome-shaped and was colored red, symbolic of war.

In the attack an attempt would often be made to take captives. These would be taken to the town and burnt at the stake right off or kept until the next annual ceremony. Here, then, they were sacrificed by being burnt in the southeast corner of the town square at high noon of the second ceremonial day, as an offering to the Sun. The shedding of human blood upon the town square shrine at this ceremonial time was, as we shall see later, quite an important rite.

Scalps were taken by removing the whole scalp, the hair of men being dressed to form one entire scalp lock covering the crown. When scalps were brought to the town, they were stretched on hoops and carried in a dance at night, by the women relatives of those who took them, as among the prairie tribes. A cry, said to be in imitation of the wolf, was given by a warrior when a scalp was taken, and the same cry is nowadays given by a player in the ball game who throws a goal. This is called the 'gobble-whoop,' as it ends in a tremulous gobble made in the throat; a very popular cry among all the southern tribes. Before going to war the town would perform all the dances and many of the ceremonies of the annual ceremony, to propitiate and secure the favor of the clan totems and other beings. This performance was called the War Dance in the common parlance of the Indians and white men.

GAMES.

With the Yuchi, all games have a strong ceremonial aspect. They are, most of them, of a public character, taking place in the allotted playground adjacent to the public square.   The afternoon of the second day of the annual festival is the usual time for playing them ceremonially.   Many of the games are accompanied by ritual, more especially the ball game.   Stakes are wagered in nearly all games by both players and spectators.   Like most Indian games the betting is a very important item of consideration.

The first to call for description is the ball game played with two rackets and known quite generally among the tribes of the Southeast. A number of descriptions of the game as played by various tribes are available and offer interesting material for comparison.[1]

This game commands more interest among the Yuchi than any other, and is always played after the emetic is taken and the feast completed, on the second day of the annual ceremony. It has been, however, played at other times of the year by different parties in the tribe or made an intertribal or intertown contest for the purpose of betting. The Yuchi have frequently played against other towns of the Creek Nation. The game is still played in a modified manner.

A rite, called the Ball Game Dance, is performed the night before, in honor of the sticks which are used in the game, and the supernatural power residing in them.   The sticks are placed on a scaffold, usually in the west lodge of the square ground, with a line of women standing behind it.   Men, including the players, are lined up on the opposite side.   They all sing and stamp their feet, but in this dance the loudest singing is done by the women . Sometimes the sticks are painted red for this ceremony, to symbolize their combative function.

As many players as wish or are fitted to do so may take part in the game, though the sides must be evenly matched.   On this occasion, men of the Chief class form one side and Warriors the other.   The latter are traditionally mean players, even nowadays resorting to foul play and violence.   Each side choses a chief or leader, and his regalia at the present day consists of a

---

[1] A compilation of much of the material has been made by Culin and published. See games of the North American Indians, in Twenty-fourth Annual Report of Bureau American Ethnology (1902–1903), p. 561, *et seq.*

cow's tail stained red, worn sticking out from the back of the belt, or a collar of red cloth having a number of blue strips hanging from it. Common players must not wear foot coverings or hats. The custom now is to have a handkerchief bound around the head. Formerly no clothing save the breechcloth and sash or cow's tail was worn.

Goals consisting of two uprights and a cross piece are erected at each end of a level stretch, about 250 feet apart. The course of the ball field is east and west. Each goal is sacred to one side, and various means are attempted to bewitch that of the opponents. If a woman with child can be made to encircle the goal of the opposite side it will cause that side to lose. In very formal games certain taboos of actions and diet were enforced, but these practices are now obsolete.

The sticks used in this game are made of hickory. Two are used by each player, that in the right hand often being longer by several inches. These ball sticks, *dagä*^{n}*cá* (Pl. VI, Fig. 2), are usually about three feet long, of heavy, well-seasoned hickory wood. They are sometimes circular, sometimes polygonal in section. The scoop to catch the ball in is formed by cutting about one foot of the shaft down flat, then turning and bending it back upon the handle end, where it is lashed fast in several places. The open scoop is then netted with rawhide or deerskin, one thong running lengthwise across the open and another crosswise. In some particularly good sticks there are two thongs each way. Holes through the rim of the scoop are made for fastening the thongs. Some variety in detail is found in different specimens. The crosswise thongs are twisted up tight, so as to hold fast the lengthwise strand which passes through the twist perpendicularly.

The ball, *dagä*$^{n\prime}$, is made of buckskin stuffed with deer hair and contains a conjured object in the center. It is about two and one-half inches in diameter, the cover consisting of two round pieces of soft deerskin sewed together all around their edges. A specimen ball, when opened, proved to contain a core of red cloth which was itself sewed up in the form of a ball. The large ball, *dagä*$^{n\varepsilon}$*ä*, used in the football and handball game, is six inches in diameter and much softer than the small one. Several auxiliary lines of stitching are put on the opposite sides of the joining seam to take up whatever slack might result from violent usage.

The other tribes using two sticks in this game, in contrast to the one-stick game of the northern Plains and Algonkian tribes, are the Creek, Seminole, Cherokee, Choctaw, Chickasaw and Shawnee. The Choctaw seem to have carried the ball game to its highest athletic and ceremonial form.

Before the Yuchi begin a game, an address of encouragement and instruction is given by an old man of the Warrior society who has charge of the event. In one form of the game the sticks are laid on the ground in a pile and at a signal the players scramble for them. At other times, time is taken up in conjuring the score-ground. An old man, a Warrior, marks a line on the ground near the ball field. He cuts small sticks to represent points or goals. Then he begins a harangue to the sticks and the mark, telling them to be fair and so on, pointing all the time at the different objects He names the sides on the line and the little score sticks. After this conjuration he takes the ball and, when the players are ready, being arranged in squads near their goals, tosses up the ball from the middle point between the goals. Then he runs to one side to escape the clash of the opponents. The players close in to catch the ball in their rackets and force it through their opponents' goal posts.

Strict care must be taken by the players not to allow the ball to be touched by their hands. This is about the only rule of the game, every sort of strategy and violence being allowed. When a player makes a goal he throws his body forward, elevates his elbows and gives the 'gobble' yell, a tremulous whoop also given as a scalp cry. This is a taunt.

From this point on the game is a wild struggle. The bystanders add to the confusion by shouting and yelling cries of encouragement, *gyä*, 'hurry up,' *kyē*, 'here,' and other directions intended to aid the players, just like white spectators. Wherever the ball is there is a pushing, shouting, yelling crowd of

Fig. 34.   Plan of Ball Field.

players trying to get it in their rackets. Those on the inside are fumbling and trying to prevent others from securing it, while those farthest away are pushing and hammering with their sticks to break a passage toward the center, until someone secures the ball and sends it up in the air over the heads of the crowd toward the opponents' goal if possible. Then someone else who has been waiting at a distance for just this occasion has time to seize the ball between his rackets and line it off for a goal before the crowd reaches him. He is lucky if he does not get clubbed by some angry opponent after this. If his throw falls short or misses the goal someone else has a chance to get it and make a throw. Or if the player who catches the ball is near the hostile goal he may try to run with the ball tightly gripped in his rackets. Then his success depends upon his speed, but his pace may be slackened by a blow from the racket of some one of his pursuers, whereupon he drops the'ball and the crush closes in about him. Or he may circle off and by outrunning the rest succeed in carrying the ball through the goal posts, while everyone sets up a yell and the sides line up with suppressed excitement for another inning.

The line-up was observed as follows: according to the number of players a certain force was placed to guard the goal post on each side, while the majority were grouped on opposite sides of the center of the ground where the ball is tossed up. Thus there were two squads on each side. Between these squads few half-way men were stationed. The diagram, Fig. 34, shows a typical arrangement, the black dots representing one side, the circle their opponents. The cross X is where the ball is tossed up. As the games observed were between members of the two societies of the tribe, the players in the figure, indicated by circles and dots, represent respectively Chiefs and Warriors.

Goals obtained are marked by the score-keeper, by driving small sticks in the ground on the side of the line which has scored. The first side to score twenty goals wins. In this game men are often seriously injured and killed. It is stated that, in a game between the Yuchi and one of the Creek towns some years ago, four men were fatally injured. The photographs (Pl. XVI.) show groups of players at different stages of a game which took place in conclusion of the annual ceremony of 1905.

A similar game in which women may take part on both sides, or against men, is played with a large ball (Fig. 35), the bare hands alone being used. This is an informal and very amusing event. Played in another way the ball is kicked by men and women on opposite sides. This was called $dag_A{}^n$ tené, 'ball kick.'

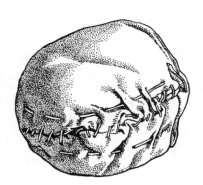

Fig. 35.   Foot Ball.

Another game is called cow's head. A cow's head is e l e v a t e d on a pole about twenty feet high, and men and women strive to hit it with a small ball, which the women throw with their hands and the men with ball sticks. Counts are as follows:

Hitting cow's head counts for men . . . . . . 1, for women . . . 5
    "   " horn   "   "   " . . . . . . 1, "   "   . . . 2
  " two feet below head "   " . . . . . . 1, "   "   . . . 1

Played in another way, the women throw the ball, which was a large one in this case, while the men kick it. Twenty players were on each side. Betting was carried on with both of these games.

Like the prairie tribes, the Yuchi women also played a game with two balls connected by a thong. This they tossed by means of a simple straight stick. There was no goal, the object merely being to get the chain ball away from the opponent. The hoop and throwing stick game was also known to the Yuchi. Cat's cradles or string games are well known by children and adults. Four or five of these string figures were seen.   One of them, for instance, was called Crowfoot,[1] another resembled the common Jacob's Ladder,[2] while the others, extremely long and complex, could not be named.   All of the figures were made by one person alone and the figures were brought out chiefly by manipulating the right hand.   A common figure was similar to that known to white children under the name of 'sawing wood.'[3]   Some of the string figures may have been learned from white people.

Horse racing, foot racing and trials of strength and endurance are greatly to the liking of the Indians.   On such occasions they usually indulge freely in betting.   Among other contests carried on by men is a form of wrestling. The first grasp is an elbow grasp, each man holding the other somewhere near the elbow and trying to throw him backwards by dexterous twisting or by combined strength and weight.   The semiformal giving of presents to guests and friends is also a fairly common practice upon the occasion of the gatherings.   The event is hardly to be called formal, as the giver simply offers tobacco to the person he wishes to honor and states aloud what he will give.   The recipient is under no obligations to return the favor until some time has passed, when he is expected to return to the giver another and more valuable gift.

[1] The finished pattern resembles "Leashing of Lochiel's Dogs" (cf. String Figures, by Caroline F. Jayne, New York, 1906, pp. 116, 120; also the Tanana " Raven's Feet") (ibid. p. 306, fig. 825) ; and the Cherokee "Crow's Feet" (cf. A. C. Haddon, American Anthropologist, Vol. V, No. 2, p. 217).

[2] This resembles an Osage figure recorded by Mrs. Jayne (cf. String Figures, p. 27, Fig. 50.)

[3] Cf. ibid. p. 357 Fig. 805.

CUSTOMS.

BIRTH.

Before child-birth takes place the prospective mother retires to a secluded temporary camp always east of the usual dwelling. Here she is attended by one or two old women relatives and her mother.

In order to facilitate delivery a decoction is made by placing a bullet in a cup of water, and the woman is given this to drink. During delivery she lies flat on her back on the floor or on the ground. Sometimes the family

Fig. 36. Objects Deposited With Navel Cord.

induces an old woman to come and help the woman in labor by sitting on her abdomen so that she can be held in her arms. As soon as the child is born it is washed, but no clothes are put on it until the fourth day, when it is named. The mother is allowed to partake of nourishment; the child, how-ever, is not given suck until the fourth day. The taboos shortly to be described which devolve upon the father go into effect as soon as the child is born.

The fetal coverings are disposed of by inhumation. Care is taken to preserve the umbilical cord. In the case of a male child it is treated in the following manner: the father has prepared a small bow about eight inches long and strung with wound sinew, an imitation of the larger weapon. Four arrows, notched but unfeathered, with sharpened shafts, accompany the bow (Fig. 35, a). The arrows are then bound, together with the navel cord, at the center of the little bow, and the whole thing is thrown where the brush is very dense and where no one will see it. This is an invocation and prayer that the boy grow up to be a masterful handler of the bow both in hunting and in war.

In the case of a female child the cord is likewise preserved. It is carried to the great log mortar which stands in the space before every Yuchi house, and tucked snugly away beneath it in the earth at the base. The father then carves a small model of a mortar and pestle together with two different sized pot-stirrers (Fig. 36, b, c, d). These objects are preserved somewhere about the house or camp and represent a prayer that the girl may grow up to be proficient in all the arts of good housekeeping. When the father is informed that his child is a boy he is pleased, and the birth of a female child brings joy to the mother.

The Yuchi do not, as far as has been observed, practice the custom of making cradle boards for their infants as some of their neighbors do. On the contrary, a hammock of cloth or of strouding is constructed upon two ropes attached to trees, and separated by two cross pieces at head and foot to spread the opening at the top and admit air to the child. When the mother wishes to carry it, the infant is either slung in a shawl upon her back, or if strong enough, is made to straddle her hip with her arm about its waist for support. Some amulets are usually fastened about its neck to protect the child from sickness. While some of the southeastern tribes followed the custom of artificially flattening the frontal region of the skulls of infants,[1] considerable inquiry among the older Yuchi people failed to bring out any definite information on this point, so it seems likely that if this was ever done by them it has long been forgotten.

Upon the birth of a child into the family certain very strict taboos fall upon the father. From the day that the child is born he may do no work, nor sleep in his customary place in the house for the space of one month. He usually establishes himself in a camp near by. A strict dietary taboo also prevents him from tasting salt, sweet potatoes, pumpkins, melons and musk melons for the same period. The stigma of religious uncleanness which attaches to the wife during the season of child-birth and catamenia, is apparently shared by the husband. During the month of taboos he is not

---

[1] Cf. American Anthropologist (N. S.) vol. 9, No. 2, p. 294 (1907).

expected to mingle much with his companions in public places, and should he attempt to ignore his bounds, they would remind him of them by shunning him or casting blame and ridicule upon him.

The actions of the father are believed to exert some sort of influence upon the growth of the child during this tender period, before it is considered to have severed all the bonds which link it with the supernatural. The child is looked upon as the reincarnation of some ancestral spirit from the spirit world. Should the father violate the taboos not only he might suffer but the child itself would pay the penalty for his transgressions. As for the rest, the community at large thinks it best to have as little as possible to do with the couple who have thus come into communication with the supernatural, since no one can tell what evil consequences may follow. As surely as the father might suffer, if he transgressed, he would be the means of spreading abroad the contagion of evil. The religious significance of the taboo in this tribe will be treated more at length in the general discussion of religious beliefs.

To the father of a family fell the lot of instructing his boys in manly exercises and in the duties and privileges of whichever of the two societies he inherited prospective membership in. The mother on her part was responsible for the training up of her daughters in domestic duties.

NAMING.

The fourth day after its birth is the all important day for the newly born child. It is then no longer a half-spirit, but a real human being and belongs to earth. Upon this day it is first given suck, and a name having been chosen by both mother and father, preparations are made to bestow it upon the infant. In regard to the choice of names there is a significant rule that a child shall take the name of some maternal grandparent's brother or sister according to sex. Thus names are transmitted in accordance to a maternal system of inheritance, and, although the clan of the individual is by no means illustrated in his name, as it is among the Creeks, Siouan, and Algonkian tribes, it is quite evident that the same names will descend through the same clan, occurring in alternate generations. Under this arrangement if all the names in a certain clan were a matter of general knowledge throughout the community, the custom would more nearly coincide with the above-mentioned groups where personal names indicate clanship. It is not uncommon, however, for children to be named directly after the totem. Although the percentage of such names is not high, they are still to be found. For example, we find *Sag^ɛē' sīné*, 'Little Bear,' to be a member of the Bear clan. In some cases, I was informed, the ancestral name is not perpetuated in the child, but the parents may if they desire invent a new name connected with some peculiarity of the child or some incident attending its birth. The usual ceremony of naming on the fourth day after birth, consists in fastening a string of white beads about the infant's neck in token of the occasion. These beads are worn continually until the child is able to walk about. In default of a string of beads a single white bead is often substituted.

The above facts regarding personal names are significant in another respect, and have something to do with the idea of reincarnation. When it is borne in mind that, in the journey of the departing soul, it requires four days to reach the land of the dead, there appears an evident connection between these four days and those that are allowed to pass before the newly born child is given its name.

The Yuchi believe that in naming a child after the ancestor it will exhibit the qualities of that ancestor, and it is frequent to hear a father remark how much his son is getting to be like his great uncle, and then proceed to eulogize the latter. The child spoken of will bear his name, often with the diminutive particle if the name is of European origin, as John, Little John. Judging by conversations that I have had with the Yuchi upon the matter of reincarnation, it seems that belief in the connection between the body and temperament of the child, and those of its maternal ancestor in the second past generation, undoubtedly exists in their minds.

Ceremonial or political position is not indicated in the name of an individual, so when such ranks are mentioned they are apart from the name. It is not known that names have been changed or multiplied, there does not seem to be any reluctance in the matter of mentioning the names of dead persons. In common use personal names are not very much heard. In fact, some people seem to be rather ashamed of them, and when questioned on the subject will refer to a bystander or some friend. Not infrequently a man when giving his name will whisper it. Particularly at the ceremonies men are addressed by their society titles, as *Bále^n*, Chief, or *Sä^{n}bá*, Warrior, *Goconé*, and so on. The characteristic features of names among the Yuchi are, in brief, that one name, supposedly indicating the reincarnation of a maternal antecedent two generations removed, is borne unvaried through life, and that nothing necessarily expressed in the name itself indicates clanship, or rank.

Following is a list of names with interpretations given by an interpreter, in some cases attainable by analysis, in others not. The interpretations lay no claim to accuracy, for many of the names themselves are regarded as archaisms.

Dasewi', ...Comes crossing.
Katané, ...Meet him.
Yalewi', ...Come back.
GΛmbesī'ne . . . . .Little screw driver.
AgΛ^{n}goné . . . . .Comes with someone (fem.).
Go'tá . . . . .Shake with something.

Ka'ká ....White man.
Fago^εoⁿwī' ....Comes out of the thicket.
Ekīlané..............It has left me.
Gopētcané ....Man who jumps over something.
Kūbá...............Creek Indian (literally, 'Looking up this way').
Dastanaⁿgī' ....For Creek, *TastAnA'gi*, warrior.
Kīlewī' ....Passing.
Gone^εä'.............Big baby.
Gēgogané............Sent back home.
Yástagolané..........Goes toward the fire (fem.).
Gaⁿsīné..............Little baby (fem.).
Gobadane' ....Sheep (literally, 'fat leg').
Go^εä' ....Big person (fem.).
Ya't̄ä^εgoⁿjé ....Gone ahead with someone (fem.).
Yáda poⁿlé ....Under the bucket
Goⁿläⁿtcīné ....Runs after him.
DjAⁿbo'..............Crooked John.
Goyá^εané.............Cuts up sticks (with an axe).
Djadjī sī'^εAⁿ ....Little George.
S^εaté ....Touches the ground.
S^εagwané ....Takes him down.
Yuwagégoⁿläⁿ' ....
Sag^εē' sīné ....Little Bear.

MARRIAGE.

Marriage among the Yuchi is remarkably simple, being attended by no ceremony so far as could be learned. A young man having found a girl to his taste in various respects, decides to appropriate her. He meets her frequently and courts her. She leaves home at length of her own will and he builds a house for them. No exchange, so far as is known, is made, but it often happened that the man gave the girl's family a pony. Sometimes the man goes to live with his wife's parents until he is able to start for himself. The couple separates at will, but the children go with the mother. Should this occur, the man must never speak to her again under any circumstances, as it would lessen her chance with other men.

There is a restriction in regard to marriage, however, that is very strict. Each individual is a member of a certain totemic group, or clan, and marriage between members of the same clan is strictly tabooed as a form of incest. The clans, however, are all equal in this respect, as marriage may take place between any two.

As a rule, it may be added, married people, if such concubinage should be called marriage, are quite sympathetic with each other.

Polygamy was practiced in the past quite generally. A man could have as many wives as he could get and keep. His residence in such a case was his own, but each wife had her own property, the children she bore belonging to her and her clan. Unfaithful wives were punished by having their ears cut off.

INITIATION.

Each boy at the time when he reaches the age of puberty is set off from his companions by certain rules of conduct. His period of initiation is brought to a culmination at the next annual ceremony performed by the tribe in the town square. During this event he, with other boys who are being initiated, has certain ceremonial offices to perform. When the ceremony is over his period of initiation is likewise over, and he is regarded as an adult, although a callow and inexperienced one. He is then in the right position to take a wife, have a voice in the town square, and receive appointment to some higher ceremonial office. Thereafter the people watch him to find some manifestation of ability in industrial, civil or military matters according to his bent. Henceforth the young man is under the guidance and protection of his clan totem, the initiation rites and adoption into the town having at the same time secured this for him. Initiation was, in brief, the formal admission of youths into the privileges of their hereditary society, and into the rank of responsible manhood in their clan and town.

Further mention will be made of the boys undergoing the last stages of their initiation term in the account of the annual ceremony, and again in the description of the public offices in the town, where they are known as *yatcigi'*.

MENSTRUATION.

During the menstrual periods, the Yuchi woman is obliged to leave the common domicile, the company of her husband and family. Going away by herself she makes a shelter some distance from the camp, usually to the east of it. Here she remains for four days, having no part in the preparation of food for the household and taking no part in any household duties whatever. She may not even touch common property, striving to be seen as little as possible by friends or relatives. A very stringent taboo was that she should sleep apart from her husband. In fact, during this whole period of about four days an atmosphere of seclusion surrounds the near relatives, while the husband refrains from joining hunting parties or social gatherings with his friends, since it is understood that his company is not desired for the time. The reason given for this is that the woman is considered to be unclean and that objects or persons coming in touch with her acquire the same quality. The uncleanness referred to is a magic not a physical quality. It is thought that she becomes a mere involuntary agent of evil magic at this time.

While the woman is thus secluded food is brought to her by her mother in four small dishes, *yadadané* (Pl. III, Fig. 1), of unbaked clay, one being for sofkee, one for meat and the others for bread and coffee. These foods are left under a tree near at hand by the woman's mother, within easy reach. Before returning to her home the woman must wash herself and all garments concerned with her. The small dishes are destroyed. This is done to obliterate all possible channels through which the power of harm might flow from the unclean to clean objects.

BURIAL.

BELIEFS.—The individual, according to Yuchi religious philosophy, possesses four spirits, *nₐⁿgᵉä'*, one of which at death remains in the spot where disembodiment took place, while two others hover in the vicinity of the tribesfolk and relatives. The information in regard to these two, however, is rather vague. The fourth starts upon a four days' journey along the rainbow trail eastward to *yūbahē'*, 'far overhead,' the haven of souls. At the point where earth and sky meet, a great cloud is constantly rising and falling. Under this cloud all souls must pass and, should the passage be made in safety, *yūbahé* is subsequently attained. But many souls are crushed and lost forever, while some are obliged to return to earth again in failing, through fear, to pass the obstacle. Those spirits which remain on earth may be propitious or otherwise, but are generally held in fear. A general belief that the reincarnation of ancestors in the maternal line takes place in the birth of children has already been mentioned.

RITES.—Upon the death of an individual the observances practiced have a twofold function: they not only manifest the grief of the survivors but they are destined to prepare the soul elements for the last journey, the trial at the end of the earth, and future existence.

The mortuary customs of the Yuchi have undergone a change within the last two decades, a change from burial beneath the house floor to outdoor burial. The same may be said of their neighbors the Creeks. In former times the rites were as follows: as soon as death had been ascertained, public announcement of it was made by the assistant of the town chief, or second chief. Six shots were, and are today, fired from a rifle to apprise both the living and the dead of the event. In the winter of 1904 when Katána, Charles Big Pond, died ten shots were fired as an especial tribute, but this was not often rendered to ordinary men. The number fired for Chiefs and Warriors is the same. The body of the man is then washed by near relatives and laid on its back upon the floor. He is dressed in good clothes and his face is painted with the Chief or Warrior design according to his society. By this time the camp is informed and general lamentation follows. Anciently it was customary for men to assemble on the ensuing morning and dig a grave directly in the center of the earth floor of the house. Both then and now boards were placed, or slabs of bark, at the bottom and around the sides of the pit, since no dirt must come in contact with the body. A package of tobacco and some money were inhumed at the same time. When burial was beneath the floor neither horse nor dog was slain over the spot, and the occupation of the house was not interrupted.

In most respects the same details in rite are followed out in the present day as in the past, but the modern rite differs in some particulars. A common burying ground is usually to be found near each point of settlement, so when a dead man has been properly attired and decorated he is carried thither and buried in the manner described before. The head is always placed to the west, causing the face to be directed toward the east, the direction in which the departing spirit journeys. Once, according to a last request, an old man was interred facing the west because, as he said, being a progressive man, disgusted with old conditions, he did not wish to travel the path of his ancestors.

A fire is built at the head of the pit and maintained for four days and nights to light up the path of the spirit. It probably has some symbolic reference to the sun also. Bread, meat, boiled corn and a bundle of clothes are laid beside the body, the food stuffs usually in an earthen bowl. The horse, or dog, or both, of the deceased were sometimes slain over the grave to serve their master, but this practice is obsolete.

When interment has been completed a volley of four rifles is discharged over the grave, as a final salute, and to clear the path for the soul, the shooters facing east. A structure composed of notched logs, or boards, in the form of a roof is erected over the spot, assumedly as a protection to the remains.

To rid the premises of the household from the possible presence of the wandering spirits, which are held in fear, a bucket is filled with cedar leaves and smudged about the house, on all sides and in the garden patch. This is done but once and considered effectual. On the morning of the fourth day, a shaman prepares a feast in the house of the dead. Its doors are thrown open and all comers are made welcome at the spread. This feast celebrates the supposed safe arrival of the spirit in the upper world.

Sickness, in the shape of rheumatic pains, is believed to fall upon any person who becomes soiled with dirt from a newly dug grave. The vicinity of a burying ground is commonly avoided as the wandering spirits are thought to abound there. Names of dead persons are not tabooed. Graves, nowadays, are not visited much or kept in repair. Lastly, there is said to be a slight difference between the mortuary rites practiced for the Chief society and those practiced for the Warrior society. The Yuchi do not seem to have special clan rites at death.

Miscellaneous Customs.

SMOKING.—Tobacco, *i*, has always been raised quite extensively by each family for smoking and for ceremonial use.

For ordinary use it has been customary to mix sumac leaves with the tobacco in varying proportions. Both men and women smoke for pleasure. It should be recalled[1] that a somewhat irregular polish was given to pipe bowls by rubbing them when wet with a piece of smooth stone. The pipe forms sometimes resemble frogs. These symbolize the frog which a supernatural being named Wind used as a pipe bowl in the mythical age. The pipe stems also symbolize a snake, which he used as his pipe stem, his tobacco being snake dung. The myth referred to will be given at the end of this paper.

Smoking is called 'tobacco drink.' Men, women and even small children practice it, though they are not by any means incessant smokers. When they do smoke, however, it is done rather vigorously with much inhaling. People smoke more in winter than in summer. Formerly, each man carried his smoking articles with him in a pouch hanging at his side.

Ceremonial smoking used to be a common observance. It added a tone of sincerity to any communications between people. Strangers were welcomed with a quiet, friendly smoke, and any matters which required deliberation, whether private or public, were thought over for a time while all were engaged in smoking. In the town square, when meetings took place, each member of the town who was present produced his pipe and tobacco while an official of the Chief society passed around among the lodges furnishing everyone with a light. Sometimes the official lighted a pipe and passed it around for each man to take a puff from it. It was believed that if one smoked while deliberating in sincerity over a question and, at the same time, entertained malice or insincerity toward it in his mind he would die. In the same way it was thought that anyone suspected of mischief or evil intentions could be detected by a challenge to smoke with the accuser. In fact it was evidently regarded as an oath and an ordeal to test veracity or guilt. The following, mentioned in one of the myths, shows the power of tobacco smoke in a case of wrong-doing.

"Now the owner of the house was an evil man. He was Iron Man. Wind knew all about that and he even knew that Iron Man had killed his four sons. Then Wind decided to kill him. When he smoked he drew in a great deal of smoke and blew it on Iron Man. And that is the way he killed him."

---

[1] See page 30.

The Yuchi take their rest at night in a very irregular way, getting up at all hours for the purpose of talking, singing, gambling, or inspecting their horses, when in camp. Nightly debauchery is common; when intoxicants abound undisturbed rest is unknown in the camps. No one attempts to remedy these faults by means of persuasion or force, except the wife of the disturber. Women have a good deal of power of this sort and, although seemingly very submissive and passive, their advice is often asked in matters of decision, while the men are patient in listening to rebukes from them. In public, women must remain in the background when their men are present. They never engage in conversation with other men in the presence of their husbands who must be spokesmen when outside communication is necessary.

Children in crawling often rest on the hands and on the soles of their feet, instead of their knees. In climbing, the men press the soles of the feet to the bark and hug the tree with the arms, raising both feet for a new grip. Boys of five or six years and upward are allowed to smoke tobacco as much as they choose. Women carry children astride the hip. Children spend much time in building mounds of dirt and playing with sticks and stones in sand or mud. Little girls have dolls of rags and deerskin which they play with.

Both men and women are, for Indians, decidedly cleanly in personal habits. Their clothes are kept carefully clean and neat. They frequently wash. To keep the teeth clean a piece of willow stick is chewed on the end until it is shredded and pulpy. This is chewed and rubbed across the teeth to remove accretions, while the sap forms a kind of suds.

Children are seldom punished for any mischief that they do. They are never whipped. If, however, it is thought necessary to give them a reminder in the shape of chastisement, a vessel of water is thrown over them.

It was not very common in the past for a girl to grow up and not be married, so there were few unmarried women. Such women, however, usually lived with different men merely as concubines, staying for a while with one, then going to live with another.

As far back as can be remembered, it was the custom for men when they met to shake hands and to offer each other some tobacco.

Old people were not ill treated. On the contrary, they were respected and served by their children. It is understood that old men are to be cared for by their sons the same today as formerly.

In regard to the temperament of the Yuchi, it seems that they were, and are today, inclined to be mild and quiet mannered. They prefer to avoid quarrels, only when they become suspicious showing a tendency to grow sullen. I think, on the whole, if there is any value in such a statement at all, that anyone accustomed to the appearance of Indians in general, would find in the Yuchi a noticeably open, pleasant, and kind expression of the face.

The Yuchi, like most Indians, are by no means apathetic in temperament. They exhibit a lively interest in their surroundings, are fairly quick in grasping ideas, and in learning new things. They show an interest, too, in the customs of their neighbors, commenting not a little on what they observe. Like good gossips, they take good care of their own and their neighbors' private affairs.

The telling of myths and tales is a favorite idle hour pastime in the camps. There do not seem to be any restrictions as to place or time of year, for I have heard them narrating myths both in summer and winter, day and night. Good narrators of stories are generally respected and looked up to by the people. They have a few peculiar mannerisms, making frequent use of pantomimic and descriptive gestures. Mention of the sun is invariably accompanied by pointing upward with the index finger. At the beginning of narratives, stereotyped phrases are commonly used, such as, "In the olden (mythical) times ....", "The old people tell it ....," "It is said that ...." and others similar. Often the tale starts in abruptly with the mention of the two chief characters, while the first few sentences point out what is to follow, like a preface. The narrative is liberally punctuated with the phrase "so they said " which takes the place of the quotative and also serves as a rhetorical pause period. The narrator always closes his account with "This is the end," "Now (then)," "Here it ends," "This is enough" or similar concluding phrases. Some short statement entirely irrelevant to the tale itself, but spoken in the same tone and without much of a break, may be appended, such as, "My name is Joseph," "I am your friend," "I am only a young man in wisdom, but I have told what I heard," "Give me some tobacco," "It is late," "The day is a bad one." The Yuchi audience is a quiet one, usually waiting until the end of a story before expressing comment. They often interrupt, however, with laughter or with "*ho ho!*", as a sign of assent.

These Indians have a few exclamatory expressions which are used in various circumstances. An expression of sudden anger, known also among the neighboring Creeks, is *áyīlà!!* The men give vent to disbelief or contempt of what another is saying by exclaiming *gū! gū'!!*; the women, by exclaiming in a high voice, *hī hₐⁿ!* A surd sound, *tck tck tck*, is a signal to frighten small children when they are up to mischief. Dogs know this signal too. It stands for "stop!" Another explosive expression, *cī!!* is commonly used to frighten dogs, but is not for persons. A signal of warning or caution, also common, is given by hissing between the tongue-tip and the base of the teeth. This means "be on your guard," "look out," "watch your chance," etc. Dogs are called by a few sharp inspiratory whistles.

The numeral system in Yuchi is a decimal one. The numbers up to ten do not yield to analysis. From ten to twenty, however, the expression is, "ten, one coming on," "ten, two coming on," etc. Twenty is literally "man (or leg) two;" thirty, "man (or leg) three," etc. One hundred is "finger-nail one," and one thousand is nowadays rendered as "finger-nail long one," or "one hundred long."

RELIGION.

Religious Beliefs and Folk-Lore.

In treating other subjects frequent mention has been made, heretofore, of various religious beliefs connected with different phases of life, of the ideas which the Yuchi hold regarding the supernatural realm, and how they maintain their relations with the latter by means of rites and ceremonies. An attempt will now be made to give as many of these beliefs as could be gotten in order to present as clearly as possible an idea of the religious life of the tribe.

In the earliest mythological time about which anything at all is known, there existed only a certain realm of water and air called *yūbahé*, 'in the far heights.' This expanse was boundless and flat. It was inhabited by beings who lived in the water and beings who lived in the air. Just what their form was is not known for all, but some of those that are mentioned have animal names and show animal characteristics, such as Crawfish, Buzzard, Panther, Spider, etc. In other respects, however, they behaved much like human beings. That many mythical animals are conceived of as human in form is indicated by the use of the particle *go*, 'human,' with their names. Others, from what we are told, who bore the names of various natural objects had animal forms too. Among these, for instance, are Sun, and Moon. It would seem, apparently, that the interest of the people in the various animals had determined the form of their deity concepts.

Others who are mentioned only by name may have been anthropomorphic. Some of these, for instance, are Sun, *Tsō*, Wind, *Wīdá*, Old Woman, *Wä^nhané*, Old Man, *Gohané*, Iron or Metal Man, *Gohä^toné*, *Gyät hä'*, the cardinal points, the four winds and others who seem not to be unlike ordinary human beings, both in their ideas and in some of their doings. The supreme deity idea, however, seems to be centered in *Tsō*, 'Sun,' who is known, as far as could be ascertained, under some different names, among them 'The One who is Breath,'[1] and 'Makes Indians' being frequent. These beings, some of them, had wives and children; they gamed, traveled about on the hunt, procreated, evidently made war and had gatherings where certain peculiar acts, which we might call rites, were performed. In short, from what we know of this mythical period of the supernatural beings, their life was much like that which the Indians lead, except that death was non-existent. There were evidently chiefs among these beings who, in a general way, might be regarded

---

[1] Comparable in sense to the Creek supreme deity and creator, Hisákidamīssī, 'Master of Breath.'

as central figures in mythology, but no one being in particular is mentioned as such. In one connection Sun is evidently chief, in another *Gohä*ⁿ*toné*, though the matter is not at all clear.

The social gatherings of these beings should be mentioned again, on account of the fact that what was done at such times by the supernatural beings was afterward taught to human beings by Sun, when the present earth and people were created, and in a way, was dramatized as an act of worship by the Indians. It seems that the beings used to assemble at the Rainbow, *yū*ᵋ*ä'*, and enact various peculiar rites. One of these performances was to scratch the people on the arm or breast with a certain instrument. This act will be referred to again subsequently. The beings evidently had dances too upon their Rainbow assembly ground.

After a time, it appears that some reason for change took possession of the supernatural beings. They decided to make another realm, an earth. According to the account, Crawfish dove to the bottom of the waters and brought up some dirt from which the earth was made and from which it grew to its present size. The various beings then took part in modifying the form of the earth, and in making improvements on it. Light of the proper sort was finally secured, after various attempts on the part of different beings, as well as darkness of the right intensity. The beings all seem to have been extremely active and powerful at this time, for they did various things to each other which left permanent marks upon them, which their descendants who still reside upon the earth retain. For instance, the chipmunk wanted to have night brought upon the earth, thus angering the panther, who jumped on the chipmunk and scratched his back. The chipmunk accordingly bears on his back to this day the marks of the scars he received. This example is taken simply to show a typical case of animal exploits in what might be termed the genesis period.

The following is a translation of the myth of the origin of the earth:

1. The Origin of the Earth.

"Water covered the face of the earth. Beneath the water they knew there was land, but they knew of no one who could get it. The flying creatures of the air were baffled. But they decided to get something to help them find it. The swimming creatures in the waters did not believe it could be done, because they knew the land was too far down. So they doubted.

Now the Crawfish was the one who claimed that he could find land. He told them to give him time. He told them to look for him in four days. Then he went down, and soon the water came up colored with mud. Everyone knew that before he had started the water had been clear. For four days they waited; on the fourth day the Crawfish came up. He was nearly dead when they picked him up, but in his claws they saw there was some earth. They carefully picked it out.   Then they made it round like a ball, but it looked very small.   Now one of the great birds had long claws, and when that bird lifted up his leg, they threw the ball of earth at him.   And when it struck him, the ball splashed and spread out, but it was very thin.   That is where the earth was made in the beginning.

Now all the creatures wanted to walk on it, but they gave instructions that no one should walk on it yet.   For four days it lay thus, growing larger and larger.   Now they wanted to have it level.   So they called for someone.   The Buzzard answered and said that he would go over the earth and stretch his wings.   That is the way he would make it level.   The Buzzard started, when they agreed to it, but he had not gone far before he became tired of stretching his wings so much.   He began to flutter and waver a great deal.   On account of this the Buzzard could not level it all.   And that is what made the mountain ridges.   Now the earth was made and they occupied it."

I also give the account of the creation of light and darkness, to furnish details for the generalized discussion.

2. Origin of Light, Sun, Moon and Stars.

"And everywhere was darkness.   The earth had been made, but there was no light.   The different animals gathered together.   They appointed a day for deliberation, to decide who should furnish light for the newly made earth. The Panther was the first.   They appointed him to give light because he runs backward and forward in the heavens from one end to the other.   They instructed him to go east and come back.   So he ran to the east and turned, crossed the heavens and went down in the west.   When he had done this and returned to the gathering he asked if it was all right.   They told him it was not. Then they appointed another.   They sent the Star (spider).   Now they told the Star to go east and come back.   The Star did as he was told.   He made a light in the east but it was too dim.   He went west and then came back to the gathering and asked them if it was all right.   Then they told him, ' "No. Your light is too dim."'   So they appointed another.   They appointed the Moon. They told the Moon to go east then come back through the sky and go down in the west.   The Moon started out as they directed.   When it was coming back it made a better light than that made by the Star, but it was not enough.   Then the Moon asked if it would do.   They said it would not.   Then they appointed another.   They chose the Sun, and told him what to do.   When the Sun came back westward it gave a good light, and when it went down it was all right. So the Sun was appointed to light the earth. and he gave an everlasting light.

Now when they told him about it, the Chipmunk wanted to have some night.   He said to them:

' "If it is daylight all the time, persons could not increase." ' He said, ' "If there is night, then people can rest from their work and procreate." '

So he urged in favor of night. They agreed with him in part, because they saw that what he said was true. And night came in, dividing up the day. Then when it was dark it was so dark that persons could not see to travel or to procreate. And they saw it would not do because creatures would not increase. So they put the Stars (spiders) and the Moon in with the night to enable people to see enough for those things, and it was all right. Thus the Chipmunk had made the night on the strength of his own senses, and they agreed and allowed it to remain.

When they said that, the Panther became angry and jumped upon the Chipmunk and caught him. He caught him by the neck and scratched him on the back. That is what made the red stripes on the Chipmunk's back, which he has yet. So the earth was lighted by the sun, moon and stars, and night came in too."

At some time not far removed from this mythical stage, the event of the creation of man took place. Whether this was during or after the creation of the earth is not known. At any rate, as explained in the myth, a woman in a vague way became the mother of a boy, who originated from a drop of her menstrual blood. This boy she carried to the Rainbow where the beings were gathered, and he was scratched by them as was customary. After several exciting events had taken place, which are not well understood, it seems that the mother was driven away with her boy. The inference is that the mother and son then fell from the sky to the earth. Henceforth he was called Sun, *Tsō,* and became the ancestor of a new race upon the new earth. In this way originated the human beings who called themselves *Tso'yahá,* 'Offspring of the Sun.' Then Sun taught his people certain ceremonies, which were to be performed to protect them from evil influences, and to honor the supernatural beings of the realm over the earth. He gave them two plants, *fᵉâdē',* button snake root (Eryngium yuccaefolium) and, *to tcáła,* 'red root' (Salix tristis (?)), which they were to steep and drink during the ceremony, to purify them. He instructed them in the scratching rite, which he had undergone, and instituted the practice, at the same time, of distributing new and sacred fire once a year at the occasion of the ceremonies, among the different human households. Sun then enjoined the people to keep up the dances and rites he had taught them, saying that once a year he would soar through the heavens over them and look down to see if they were obeying. He conditioned their prosperity upon their obedience and left them after giving other instructions regarding ceremonial details and features of town life. Among other things he showed them how to make an assembly ground like the one in the supernatural world and taught them how to decorate this to symbolize the Rainbow. As there are some details in this assembly ground, or town square with its symbolism, which deserve attention, it will be taken up later on. The ceremonies which were begun on earth at this time will be also described under a special heading.

It should be mentioned here that at certain times since the origin there have been born individuals with a very dark shade of skin. These black-skinned Yuchi, as they are termed, are looked upon as being more closely related to Sun than the rest of the people. They are said to be his direct offspring, their mothers having become pregnant by Sun. As no particular rank is given them, however, their position is a sort of empty aristocracy. Several black-skinned Yuchi are said to be living today, but I have not been fortunate enough to see them.

Here are several translations of variants of the origin myth which has just received comment.

3. The Origin of the Yuchi and the Ceremonies.

" The Sun deity was in her menstrual courses. She went to dip up some water (up in the sky world). She went down to the creek. Then some blood fell on the ground. She looked at the water. When she reached the top of the hill she set it down. She thought that something had happened. She went down the hill again. A small baby was sitting there. She took it along with her and kept it. She raised it and it grew. That was an Indian. She took him to the Rainbow where the others were and he was scratched and it was the ceremony at the square-ground. In the ancient time he was scratched. The drops of blood fell and lay on the ground. She placed him on the ground. The drops of blood were lying on the ground. She put him on the ground. Then she walked away from the square-ground with him, going toward the east. She reached the edge of the square. Indians came along following them. The lightning struck and frightened them. It drove them back. The Sun mother went on home with the boy. Then he went to sleep. As he grew up he became lonesome. He had no one to play with; he had no one to look at. He was lonesome. While he was sleeping and lying there, his mother pulled out one of his ribs. While he was lying there she took it out. She made a woman out of it. Then the boy awoke. He saw her. He was glad now. Then they multiplied and increased in numbers.

The Red root (*to tcālá*) and Button Snake root (*fᵉâdē'*) standing near, (which had been used when the boy was scratched and made to perform the ceremony among the sky people), she told him to use. It was made for that use. And the Yuchi are using it yet just as he told them. It is here yet. This is his medicine. While they try to keep up the ceremony and use of the medicines God (*wētânᴀ'*) goes with the people. Her son was the child of the Sun, that is what the Yuchi are named, Children of the Sun.

On that day no trouble comes to the people when they have taken the medicines. When the Sun comes up he looks down to see if they are doing the ceremonies. If he comes up high here and sees no Indians performing the ceremonies on the earth at high noon, he would stop. He would cry. It would be the end of peacefulness. The Sun would cover his face with his hands and go down again in the east. Then it would become dark and the end. It has been declared so. This is what we heard in the past."

4. Origin of the Yuchi. (Second Version.)

"There was a Sun and there was a Moon. Then the Moon was in her menstrual courses. When she got up, a drop of the blood fell from her and descended to the earth. The Sun saw it. He secured it and wrapped it up, laying it away thus for four days. On the fourth day he went and got it, and unwrapped it. When the bundle was opened, he saw that it had turned into a human being. Then he said:

' "You are my son. You shall be called *Tsōyahá.* " ' And he gave him the name *Tsōyahá*, Sun people or Offspring of the Sun. From him all the Yuchi had their origin.

Now his descendants increased until they became a powerful people. They are weakening now, but if they ever disappear from the earth a terrible thing will happen. For the Sun said:

' "If the Yuchi perish, I will not face this world. I will turn my face away, and there will be darkness upon the earth, and it will even be the last of the earth." '

So it will come to pass if all the Yuchi die out. But now there are certain Yuchi who are known to be sons of this Sun. Whenever one of them dies the Sun turns his face away from the earth for a little while. That accounts for the eclipse. These Yuchi may be known by the color of their skin, which is nearly black. The black-skinned Yuchi are the Sun's sons. There are a few living now."

In tracing this mythical history of the Yuchi we have now reached the period when human beings and the other animals seem to have been on close terms of intimacy on the earth. Everywhere magic was in operation. Animals often acted in a most offhand manner, from that moment the act becoming a rule on earth, or the result of the act becoming a natural fixity. Some specimen accounts will be given later.

A trickster appears among the animal beings by the name of Rabbit. There are other tricksters too, but Rabbit is the chief figure among them. This period is thought, roughly speaking, to have directly preceded the present one. There are many myths relating the deeds of animals and human beings which are concerned with magic. The details of the magical transformations and exploits of the earthly beings are a little too extensive to discuss here, but will be found further on under mythology.

Toward the end of this period, in short, the things of the earth and the affairs of human beings take on a more modern aspect. Many new things are originated. Death is brought to man by the disobedience of someone. Tobacco is originated from human semen. Other Indian tribes are brought into existence. Fire is secured and distributed among the people by Rabbit, and various other cultural features of human life, as well as characteristic traits among animals, are brought into existence. Some representatives of this class of myths will be given at the end of the discussion of mythology.

Up to this point we have only attempted to deal with the beliefs concerned with the supernatural beings, and with the native concepts of origin and transformation. Some of the beliefs in connection with customs and rites will now be taken up. It has already been stated, under customs, that the newly born child is believed to be the reincarnation of its predecessors. And it was shown, at the same time, that the reincarnated spirits revived in the children the qualities which they possessed during their lives. The abode of the spirits of the dead is in the sky world or the supernatural world. The path to this lies over the rainbow, and the direction to be traveled is eastward. When the soul has passed the obstacle of the swaying cloud, which is likely to crush the journeying soul and destroy it, it joins with the other spirits and supernatural beings inhabiting this realm. One of the supernatural beings, *Wăⁿhané*, Old Woman, has charge over the souls here and in some way is thought to control re-birth and the return of souls to earth. There is mention in one of the myths of some men who traveled to Old Woman and at last succeeded in obtaining the souls of their dead wives, returning to earth with them. It has also been shown how the different individuals of the clans inherited the protection of their clan totems, when they passed the initiation rites, thenceforth retaining these as protectors through life. As the members of clans are considered to be the descendants of their totemic animal, they are in a sense the cousins, as it might be expressed, of the earthly animals who are also descendants of the supernatural animals. The clan taboos and incidental beliefs need not be repeated again here as they have been mentioned in dealing with customs and the clans. But the animals of the earth, in general, are considered as thinking beings, with interests in life, customs and feelings not unlike those of men. Even today these mutual elements in the lives of men and animals are felt to exist. But naturally in the mythical age the two were more nearly on the same level than now. For, they say, it is very seldom nowadays that men and animals can converse together. A few random tales referring to such instances of recent intercommunication, however, are as follows.

An old and decrepit Indian told the story. He was complaining about his infirmities, squeaking voice, and shrunken form. He said, "I was going along on my pony late in the afternoon.   Pretty soon I came to what was like a large rock.   I heard a voice from somewhere say, " 'It smells just as though there was an old woman riding around here.' "   I looked up and saw a big rattlesnake sitting on the rock, coiled.   His neck was as thick as a man's neck.   He was looking right at *me*."

An outlaw, who was hiding from the vengeance of the relatives of the man whom he had murdered, became very hungry.   He rode up to a house and was going to ask for food.   First he crept through a cornfield near the cabin, to see if the way was safe.   While lying between the furrows there, he heard two hens talking.   They were casting glances at him.   He listened to what they were saying.   They chuckled a little, then one said, "Isn't that the fellow who is scouting around here for having killed somebody?"   The outlaw got out.

The animals are all believed to have their protecting supernatural kinsmen as well as men, for that reason in hunting them their protecting spirits have to be overcome before one can hope to bring them down.   It is the same with human beings.   If one's guardian spirit is all right no harm can come.   So in warfare, the idea is to strengthen one's own guardian kinsman spirit and to weaken the enemy's.   In this respect hunting and fishing are much like warfare.   The magic songs and formulas fight the supernatural struggle and open the way, while the actual weapons do the work when the spiritual barriers are removed.

As regards the objects in nature in general which surround them, the Yuchi have the usual animistic concepts so characteristic of the beliefs of nearly all primitive people.   Inanimate objects, and even abstract ideas such as cardinal points and various feelings and deeds, are the abodes of agencies which we may call spirits.   These may be either favorable or unfavorable to men, their. influence being believed to be largely controlled by man's personal conduct in the observance of taboos and in the performance of the rituals and ceremonies.   Plant spirits are highly powerful and important, according to the ideas of an agricultural people like this, and we shall find them to be quite prominent objects of worship in the ceremonies.

The sacred number standing out prominently in religious matters will be seen to be the number four.   Five appears less frequently.

FOLKLORE.—Here are a few miscellaneous beliefs which were recorded in regard to the natural, supernatural, and animal world.   They are given about as they were told by the Indians.

"If a terrapin in his travels walks around a big tree it is a very bad thing for him.   He will dry up.   That's why they never do it."

"The thunder or rain kills snakes.   When a storm comes up they must all go back into the ground.   If they do not, they will be killed.   So if they are killing a calf (sic!) or anything, they must leave it as soon as it begins to thunder or rain."

"When wild turkeys gobble the lightning bugs come up out of their crops. They are like little white things (maggots) before they come out."

The stars are all spiders.

Regarding the eclipse they say:—"The toad starts to eat up the moon. Then he gets big. The moon diminishes. But we frighten him away and after that the moon recovers and gets big."

One informant stated that thunder and lightning are caused by a great black snake with rattles on its tail. A being named *Ko^{n}sá no^{n}wĭ'*, the meaning of which is uncertain, rides on its back. The snake dives in and out of the water. At each flash of its wet sides there is lightning and when it rattles there is thunder.

"There was a big water vessel in the sky. Someone jerked it and spilled the water over its edge. That is what made the rain."

"Someone (a supernatural agency) in the north was trying to do something. He put some corn meal into a sifting basket and sprinkled it through. When this falls upon this earth it is snow."

"When the rainbow stretches across the sky the rain is prevented from falling through. This stops the rain and brings dry weather."

When threatened with a drought they believe that the people could cause rain to fall if they made medicine and took an emetic.

Earthquakes are believed to be caused by a being who lives in the bowels of the earth. He sometimes shakes and jerks the earth to find out how much water there remains on it.

Twins and deformed or abnormal children are believed to be sent directly by the supernatural beings to be guides to the people. They were never killed but were treated with care and raised for the public good. It is also said that when twins are born in the town it is a sign from the supernatural beings that they want to see the people improve in the performance of their religious rites.

Little people like dwarfs are believed to inhabit certain places in the dense woods. They are the souls of bad people who die, and they possess the power of killing those who either accidentally or deliberately intrude upon their haunts.

When a man sneezes, the belief is that his beloved is thinking about him. Likewise when a woman sneezes it is a sign that her lover is thinking about her.

Warts on the skin, or moles, indicate that there is too much blood or bad blood in the body. A person having them is said to need scratching until the blood flows. Moles come from bad food, too.

"When the coyotes or wolves howl it is a sign that snow or rain is coming. They can feel when a storm is approaching, and because they don't like it they start howling."

A certain kind of fish called "drumfish" is believed to have two stones in the back of its head, with which it makes a thumping noise frequently heard coming from the water when everything is quiet.

The Symbolism of the Town Square.

We shall now return again to the subject of the town square because the religious ceremonies to be described in the following pages are inseparably connected with it.

The public square-ground, where all civil and religious events of the town take place, has a symbolical significance which is quite important, and comparable in some respects to the altars and shrines of the southwestern and plains tribes.

In its ceremonial aspect the town square is symbolically a rainbow. For, according to the myth of the origin of the Yuchi and their cult, as already given, the mother of the Sun took him to the ceremony of the upper world where he was scratched. This took place on the Rainbow, *yūᵋä'*, so the present square-ground is called '*yūᵋä'*,' 'rainbow.'

The officials at the ceremonies are hence called *yūᵋähobále*ⁿ, 'rainbow or square-ground Chief' and *yūᵋähosa*ⁿ*'ba*, 'rainbow or square-ground Warrior.' The square might well be termed a rainbow shrine. Another name for the square is *sä*ⁿ*sä*ⁿ*'*, 'thoroughly beautiful' or 'good all over.'

While investigations were being made in regard to the square-ground, the assistant of the town chief brought in a colored representation of it showing how the square looked when it was formally arranged for the ceremonies. This sketch is reproduced in Plate XI. The explanation of the colors is as follows: The whole figure represents the rainbow. The brown square represents the earth. The fire in the center typifies the sun and is painted red. The ashes are represented by yellow. The three yellow lines are paths to the north, west and south lodges respectively, are likewise composed of ashes scattered by the four *yätcigī'* after the new fire has been started on the first day of the rites. This feature is now obsolete. The logs of the new fire are green, symbolizing vegetation. The brush roofs of the lodges are also green.

It will be noticed that the Warrior lodges, north and south side, have their uprights and beams colored red. This color symbolizes the Warrior class and war which they represent. The custom of coloring the posts is also now obsolete. The Chief lodge lacks this coloring. As will be seen in the photographs of the ceremonies (Plate XII, *et seq.*), a white face is given to these upright posts in modern times, by peeling off part of the outer bark and exposing the white inner surface. White is symbolical of peace.

The serpent figure lying before the north Warrior lodge is the *dätoᵋä'*, a supernatural horned serpent, and the object of veneration in the *Dätoᵋä' ctī*, now called Big Turtle Dance. This stuffed deerskin effigy was colored blue, with two yellow horns on its head. It rested in former times before the north Warrior lodge where the two Warrior officials, *goconé* and *yuᵋähosä*ⁿ*'ba*, sat with their feet upon it, but its use has been abandoned.

Something should be said here of the other meaning of the word *yūᵋä'*. Besides meaning rainbow, it stands for 'big house.' This we find to be the name given by the neighboring Creek Indians to their town square (*djógo łákko*, big house).[1]

If any credence is to be given to the statements of the Yuchi in this matter, the Creeks borrowed nearly the whole of the annual ceremonies of the Yuchi when they overran the Southeast, subduing and incorporating the latter. The modern Creeks, however, although recognizing the general similarity between their ceremonies and those of the Yuchi, do not subscribe to this opinion but claim an independent supernatural source for them.

CEREMONIES.

The ceremonies, which according to tradition originated in the other world and were taught to the first Indians by Sun, consist of various religious rites performed in public by all the men of the town once a year. The rites include dancing, fasting, the observance of certain taboos, the kindling of a new and sacred fire, the scarification of men, the taking of an emetic and the performance of the ball game. The ceremony as a whole was called, *Yūᵋāhẽ'*, 'In the rainbow,' or 'In the big house.' The time for these ceremonies is determined by the state of maturity of the corn crop. They are begun so as to coincide with its first ripening, usually about the middle or early part of July. It would seem from this that the importance of agriculture as a feature of life had determined the time for the town's discharge of its religious obligations. As far as is possible the time is also arranged so as to fall upon nights when the moon is full. This matter rests entirely in the hands of the town chief. He distributes bundles of tally sticks, one to be thrown away each day (Fig. 37), to the heads of families.

DANCES.—The special dances, *ctī*, performed by the Yuchi are quite numerous. A fairly large number are primarily clan dances, having for their object the placation of clan totems. The dancers imitate the motions of the totemic animal with their bodies and arms. The steps, however, are not subject to much variation. The dancer inclines his body forward, gesticulating with his arms according to the occasion, and raises first one foot then the other slightly above the ground, bringing them down flat at each step with vigor. In this way the dancers in single file circle contra-clockwise about the fire in the center of the square. The whole is done in a sort of run, the acoustic effect being a regularly timed stamping sound. The dances are accompanied by singing on the part of all the men dancing, and by musical instruments of several different varieties, namely, terrapin shell rattles (Pl. VII), drum (Fig. 32) and hand rattle (Pl. VII). Both the music and the instruments have been briefly described before. A few other ceremonial paraphernalia used particularly in

---

[1] Cf. the Creek Indians of Taskigi Town, Speck, in Memoirs of American Anthropological Association, Vol. II, part 2, p. 112.

the dances will be described soon.   As a rule all men may take part in any dance.   But in most of the dances only certain women are admitted from the beginning and they are provided with the bunch of terrapin shell rattles, *tsontá*, (Pl. VII) which are fastened to their legs.   During the last half of the dance, however, the exclusive feeling leaves, and women, children and even strangers may join in.   It is understood, though, that when a certain dance is being performed, for instance the Tortoise dance, the members of that clan are in the position of hosts to the others, taking pride in having them dance the dance to their totem.

The dance songs consist chiefly in the repetition of meaningless syllables or groups of syllables.   A great deal of magic potency is believed to rest in mere words and burdens.   Sometimes, however, an intelligible stanza or sentence appears having some vague reference to the object of the dance, or simply naming it.   The feeling of the dancers seems to be that they are for the time in the actual form of the totem, and they carry out in quite a realistic way the effect of the imitation entirely by their motions and behavior.   No imitative costumes nor masks are used now, nor could it be ascertained whether they ever existed.   They imitate very well, however, the cries of the animals which are being dramatized.

Besides those dances which are functionally clan dances, there are others which are addressed, as a form of worship and placation, to various animals which furnish their flesh or parts for the use of man.   Then there are also others which are directed to the spirits of animals which have the power of inflicting sickness, trouble or death upon the people.   These are imitative, similar in general appearance to those already described.   The spirits dominating certain inanimate objects are invoked in others.

Lastly, we find a miscellaneous few which are claimed to be chiefly danced for pleasure.   There has no doubt been considerable borrowing going on among the Indians and local interpretations may have been given to various dances different from their original ones.

Most of the dances are performed at night, thus filling in the time of the ceremonies with constant activity.

A list of these special dances, and the instruments used in them, is here given.

Dance.		Musical Instrument.
Ba'tä' ctī ....Horse dance		Rattle, drum.
Wedīnéⁿ ctī...........Cow	"	?
Wedīngá ctī.. ....Buffalo	"	Rattle, drum.
Däto^εä' ....Turtle	"	Rattle.
Cū cpá ctī.............Pike	"	Rattle, drum.
Cū dj^εá ctī ....Catfish	"	Rattle, drum.
Späⁿsī' ctī............Quail	"	Rattle.

	Dance.	Musical Instrument.
Wĕtcᵋä' ctī	Turkey dance	?
Kyä^n' ctī	Owl "	Rattle.
Yᴀ^ntī' ctī	Buzzard "	Rattle, drum.
Wĕtcᵋä' ctī	Chicken "	Rattle, drum.
Cäne' ctī	Duck "	Rattle, drum.
Sᵋolä^n' ctī	Lizard "	Rattle.
Wĕtsakowᴀ^n' ctī	Opossum "	?
Djätiᴀ^n' ctī	Raccoon "	Rattle, drum.
Yūsᴀ^n' ctī	Skunk "	?
Yät̆ᵋä' ctī	Gun "	Firearms.
Gocpī' ctī	Negro "	?
Yacá ctī	Leaf "	Rattle.
łaká ctī	Feather or Corn dance	Two rattles.
Tsebé^n bené ctī	Crazy or Drunken dance	Rattle.
Yo^nctá ctī	Shawnee dance	Drum.

FASTING AND TABOOS.—Fasting and the observance of certain taboos are special features of the annual ceremony. From the beginning of the event no salt is to be used by anyone. Sexual communication is also tabooed. A general fast must be kept by all the men for twelve hours before taking the emetic, that their systems may be the more receptive to purging. During the second day of the ceremony the men may not leave the town square, nor are they permitted to sleep or lean their backs against any support when tired. For the purpose of enforcing this the four young initiates are provided with poles to strike offenders with. On the second day also no women, dogs or strangers may step over the edge into the square, the women and dogs under pain of being struck by the initiates and strangers under pain of being staked out naked in its middle. The thoughts of the people, too, are expected to be turned toward supernatural things in order to please the various spirits.

NEW FIRE RITE.—The new fire rite performed at sunrise of the second day, is symbolic of a new period of life for the tribe. As far as could be learned, the fires of the various household hearths are not extinguished as among the Creeks, since the kindling of the new fire by the town chief is symbolical of this and suffices for all. The ceremonial method of starting this fire was explained before, so it need not be repeated. The logs in the center of the square-ground were ignited from the fire started in the punk and kept burning until the ceremony is over, by the proper official. The firemaking implements were kept in a bag which hung during the ceremony, along with the rattles when not in use, on the middle post at the front of the town chief's lodge, just over where he sat.

SCARIFICATION.—The next rite to be performed in public after the kindling of the fire is the scarification of the males. Every male in the town is expected to come before two pots of steeped medicinal plants, the *f*^ε*âdē'*, button snake root, and *to tcalá*, red root, and be scratched by a certain official on the arm or breast, allowing the blood to flow and drop upon the square-ground. There is an analogy between this earthly human ceremony and that enacted by the beings of the sky world. In the same way that Sun was taken to the rainbow and scratched till his blood fell upon the ground, do the Yuchi bring themselves and their male children to have their blood drawn. It seems to be regarded as a form of torture and induration to pain. The falling of their blood upon the square-ground is symbolical of the falling of the mother-of-Sun's blood upon the ground, from which the first Yuchi was created. There is another side to this scratching ceremony. It is also a purgative. The instrument used in it consists of a quill fastened to a piece of the leaf of *f*^ε*âdē'*, one of the sacred plants, set with six pins, or, as was formerly done, with garfish teeth (Fig. 40). This scratcher is dipped in a pot containing a brew of the sacred plants before each male is scratched. Thus he is inoculated with the sacred plant juices and his blood is purified by them against sickness.

THE EMETIC.—The next and perhaps the most important rite of the occasion is the taking of an emetic by all the males of the town. This practice was also instituted by Sun. He gave the people two plants, *f*^ε*âdē'* and *to tcalá*, as is recorded in the myth, and showed them how to steep them in water. He instructed them to drink the concoction to purify their bodies against sickness during the ensuing inter-ceremonial year. It is thought, in particular, that to eat the first corn of the season without having taken the emetic would certainly result in sickness inflicted by the unappeased deities. The town chief has charge of the preparation of the emetic, aided by the four boy initiates. The pots containing the concoction are of a special form with a decoration on the rim representing the sun (Fig. 31, No. 21). These pots stand during the ceremony, east of the fire near the center of the square (see diagram, Fig. 38). When the sun is about at the zenith those who are highest in rank came forward, facing the east, and drink quantities of the medicine. They are followed by the rest lower in rank and so on. Four at a time are allowed to drink. Then all await the effects quietly in their proper places in the lodges. The proper moment arriving, they proceed to a space near the square and allow the emetic to have its full effect. The rite is repeated several times. After this all the townsmen go to water, wash off their paint and return to their places about the square.

The ceremony of the emetic is concluded with a feast of the first corn and smoking. After this the ball game is played with betting. This event has been described under the heading of games. Dancing again fills in the intervening time until another round of the medicine drinking was performed. The ceremonies were then concluded.

Possibly the main object of the annual festival is the placation of every possible animus. Obedience to the commands of Sun was also highly considered as a matter of importance. Other objects of the ceremonies are, as explained, to turn the public attention to spiritual affairs for a time, away from everyday pursuits. All the potentially malicious spirits and animal, fish and vegetable spirits are propitiated or thanked as the case might be. And all personal grievances among townsmen are declared cancelled after the emetic had been taken. They furthermore state that the scratching and the emetic teach the men to inure themselves to pain and discomfort. Both rites were practiced before going to war.

Captives were, it is said, sometimes burnt to death as sacrifices to the supernatural brings during the ceremonies. In recent times a stake was erected in the southeast corner of the square at the beginning of the event, to represent the place where captives were thus treated. After the emetic is over this stake is thrown down.

The foregoing account is a very general one. A more detailed account of the ceremonial performances as witnessed by me several times will now be given. They were performed at the Sand Creek settlement, where there is a square-ground, in July, 1904, and July, 1905. The photographs were made during the 1905 celebration. There is some difference in detail between the ceremonies of Sand Creek town and Polecat town. The one here recorded is entirely that of Sand Creek town, which has since discontinued its celebration on account of disorder and violence among the young men, due to intoxication.[1] A few features of the Polecat celebration which are based on description, will also be given as they seem to have been left off by the other settlement. It may frequently be necessary to repeat something that has already been mentioned, but this is done intentionally in order to give the details of the particular case and make the account of the actual occurrences more uniform.

The Annual Town Ceremonies.

The following account of the annual ceremony of the Sand Creek Yuchi is based upon notes made at the time, and upon incidental information derived from participants. It deals chiefly with the 1905 celebration although there was no appreciable difference between that of 1904 and the event of 1905.

The Preliminary Day.—According to the evidences of maturity observable in the corn in the neighboring fields, and the approaching phase of the moon, the town chief or head priest (Jim Brown) appointed and announced,

---

[1] In 1908, on my last visit, I learned that the chiefs had decided to continue the ceremonies as usual.

to the townspeople scattered throughout the neighboring district, a day of
general assembly, at which small bundles of sticks about two inches in length
(Fig. 37) were distributed to the heads of families. The number of sticks in the
bundles indicated the number of days that should pass before the ceremonies
would take place. The day had already been decided upon by the chief and was
announced at this preliminary meeting. A stick was thrown away each morning thereafter until but one remained, and that was the day of the next assembly
at the public square. Dancing took place at this meeting to give a little practice
to the men, as they said. Arrangements were also made for the repair of the
lodges, and the obtaining of the beef for the barbecue which was to close the
event. In other words, this meeting was purely preparatory. All the top
earth was carefully taken from the square and placed in a heap behind the
north lodge.

When the day arrived for the formal celebration to commence, the Yuchi
took care to be on hand before nightfall at the public square, which was situated
in a permanent locality near Scull Creek, where a beautiful spring of clear water
flowed from a side hill. The ceremony this time was to last three days and

Fig. 37.   Tally Sticks.

to include the following ritualistic events. The first day was to be a general
gathering, with the commencement of the fast and dancing all through the first
half of that night. On the second day, the new fire ceremony was to take place
after sunrise, followed by the preparation of the medicines, the scarification,
the taking of the emetic, the breaking the fast, and the ceremonial ball game.
The ensuing night was to be given up to all-night dancing. On the third
day, the people were to disband for a while and return again, after a rest, for
several subsequent days of minor observances. This was the plan given out
for the carrying on of the celebration.

An explanatory diagram of the square-ground showing some of the things
mentioned in the following description is given (Fig. 38) and will be frequently
referred to in the account. The date of the 1904 ceremony was July 17; that
of 1905 was a few days later in the same month.

FIRST DAY.—About one hundred Yuchi having arrived, upon the day set
aside in the preliminary gathering, at the camping ground surrounding the
public square, friendly intercourse was held among the townsfolk, and sump-
tuous preparations were made for the evening meal, after which no food could
be eaten by adults until the ceremony of taking the emetic was over.

Before dark the four *yătcigī'* went out in single file toward the woods east to secure the four logs for the new fire, to be started the next morning, and also to dig the two medicine roots, *fᵉâdē'* and *to tcalá*, and to secrete them where they could be readily found when they were to be brought in. Before appearing at the camp on their return, they whooped four times to apprise the town of the commencement of the ceremony and the fast. This whooping caused quite a little commotion among the people. Their manner changed

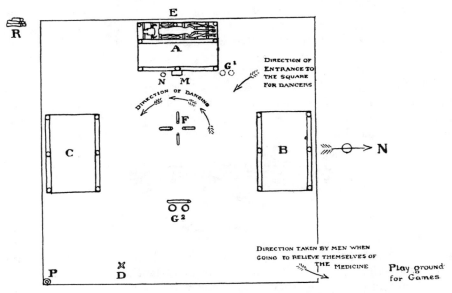

Fig. 38.   Yuchi Square-Ground During Ceremony.

A. Chief's Lodge.   M. Town Chief's Seat.
B. C. Warriors' Lodge.   N. Drum.
D. Place Where Turtle Dance Begins.   P. Stake at S.E. Corner.
E. Steer Flesh on Scaffold.   R. Pile of Wood for Fire.
F. Fire Place.
G¹. Pots of Medicine Before Ceremony of Emetic.
G². Pots During Ceremony of Scratching and Emetic.

and it seemed as though they were under constraint. The spirits of the summer ceremonial were then supposed to be watching them for infringements of the taboos. Salt and the other things spoken of before were tabooed from this time until the end of the celebration. The four logs were then deposited in the west lodge, where the Chiefs and their paraphernalia reposed.

At about ten o'clock in the evening, the moon being at the first quarter and over the west lodge, the town chief's assistant, who will hereafter be called second chief, and the *goconé* or master of ceremonies from the Warrior Society, called in a loud voice to the town to come to dance. Meanwhile the *goconé* had started a fire of fagots in the center of the square, where the fire is always made (see diagram, Fig. 38). When the lodges were filled with the townsmen, the *Dätoᵉä'* or Big Turtle Dance was begun.

THE BIG TURTLE DANCE.—In loose order, the leader having a hand rattle in his right hand, the dancers grouped themselves in the southeast corner of the square. (See diagram.) All formed in a compact mass and the leader in the center began moving in a circle, rattling and shouting *'hó! hó!'* The dancers kept in close ranks behind him echoing his shouts. After about five minutes of this, the leader started toward the fire and the dancers all held hands. A woman having the turtle shell rattles on her legs came from the northwest corner and took her place behind the leader holding hands with him. In single file the latter led them around the fire, sunwise. In 1905 there were two of these women. When the men whooped they were joined by two more, when they whooped again the women left the line. After circling a number of times the leader stopped, stamped and whooped and the ranks broke up, the dancers dispersing to their various lodges about the square. The first song was thus finished. After a short interval a leader stepped toward the fire and circling it alone started the second song and was soon joined by other dancers. Two or more women having the shell rattles on their legs took part. During the course of the next few songs the leader took the line to each of the four corners of the square, led them around in a circle and then back to the fire. No drumming accompanied this dance. Women joined in as well as children and strangers. This dance was continued for about two hours, at intervals, and was the only one danced on this night. (See Plate XII[1].)

During the process of this dance, and in all the others too, the *goconé* exhorted the dancers to their best by shouting out encouragement, and with his long staff went about to secure song leaders during the intervals of rest. The Thunder was frequently invoked this night by the *goconé* with cries of *Pīctanᴀⁿ'! Pīctanᴀⁿ'!* "Thunder! Thunder!"

At about midnight when things had quieted down a little, the town chief rose from his seat near the center of the west lodge, and silence was rendered him as he began a speech lasting about fifteen minutes. In this he referred to their ancestors who handed the ceremonies down to them; to the deities who taught them; to the obligations of the present generation to maintain them. He complimented the dancers, referred to the rites of the next day and called

---

[1] When the first flashlight (Pl. XII, 2) was discharged in making these exposures some of the dancers stopped and some went right on, but they seemed greatly startled and for a moment blinded. Several chiefs then came over and expressed their displeasure. They called it "lightning." I explained that no harm was meant and finally got their consent to make another (Pl. XII, 1) somewhat nearer.

for the assent and cooperation of his town. The men then shouted '*hó! hó!*' the sign of approbation. The town chief concluded with an appeal for good behavior and reverence during the celebration, exhorting them when the event was over to go to their homes in peace and to avoid getting into trouble or disputes with anyone. Then all dispersed for the purpose of sleep or carousing.

SECOND DAY.—Before sunrise of the second day the town chief took his seat in the west lodge. Now the four *yätcigī'* passed off toward the east to bring in the medicine plants. During their absence the town chief was preparing the flints and steel for the new fire. The return of the *yätcigī'* was announced by a series of whoops ('*hâyo! hâyo!*') and they came in with the plants, depositing them in the west lodge.

NEW FIRE RITE.

The fireplace had been swept clean and covered with sand. The *yätcigī'* now walked sunwise around the spot three times, then stopped, each one  standing at one of the cardinal points. They deposited the four logs with their ends pointing toward the cardinal points thus 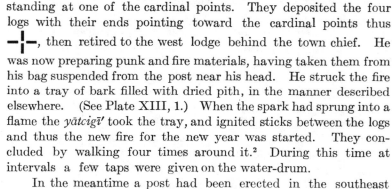, then retired to the west lodge behind the town chief. He was now preparing punk and fire materials, having taken them from his bag suspended from the post near his head. He struck the fire into a tray of bark filled with dried pith, in the manner described elsewhere. (See Plate XIII, 1.) When the spark had sprung into a flame the *yätcigī'* took the tray, and ignited sticks between the logs and thus the new fire for the new year was started. They concluded by walking four times around it.[2] During this time at intervals a few taps were given on the water-drum.

In the meantime a post had been erected in the southeast corner of the square as a sign that women, dogs and aliens, also those who have eaten corn that season or tasted food since the previous evening, were prohibited from the square under penalty of violence at the hands of the *yätcigī'*. It is also said that in war times captives were bound to this stake when they were to be burned to death.[3]

Fig. 39.
Medicine
Pounder.

---

[2] At this time in the cognate Creek and Cherokee ceremony, each family swept its hearth and started a new fire from the public embers, but the Yuchi symbolized this for the whole town by their public new fire. (19th Report Bureau American Ethnology, p. 402; Cherokee Myths, Mooney; Gatschet, Creek Migration Leg., Vol. II, p. 189 for Kasiχta town; Speck, Creek Indians of Taskigi Town, p. 142 for Taskigi town.)

[3] Also noticed by Bartram among Creeks (cf. Bartram's Travels, p. 518), but in that case there were four stakes, one at each corner of the square.

The medicine plants, red root, *to tcałá*, and button-snake root, *f^ɛâdē'*, were now brought by the *yătcigĭ'*, who walked around the fire with them five times, and then lay them lengthwise, with roots to the east and foliage to the west, in a space about fifteen feet east of the fire, where a halved log was laid on which to crush them.   Two crocks, formerly pots of a high shape, were brought full of water and stood in front of the medicines.   Kneeling before the pots the *yătcigĭ'* pounded up the roots and stems with pounders about fourteen inches long, made from peeled branches (Fig. 39).   (See Plate XIII, 2.)   The crushed roots were then put in the crocks while the stems were thrown behind the north lodge, with the pounders, upon the heap of sacred debris there.

Fig. 40.   Scratcher.

SCARIFICATION RITE.

The implement used in the scratching operation which now followed was made by the town chief of a leaf of *f^ɛâdē'* and a shaved turkey quill, having six pins fastened with their points projecting through it.   (Fig. 40).

The town chief then scratched the scratching official, *gondīné* or *yatsá*, on the right arm after some of the *f^ɛâdē'* had been rubbed over it.   The operator held the victim by the wrist, and tore his arm almost from elbow to wrist with the six-pointed instrument to the depth of one-eighth of an inch at least. No evidence of pain was manifested by anyone.   The scratcher then performed the operation on the town chief.   The Chiefs then had their turn, followed by the Warriors.   (See Plate XIV.)   Small male children were then brought up by their fathers and scratched on the arms, having also some of the medicine rubbed on their mouths. The young men came next, then the older, until all had been tortured but the four *yätcigī'*, who were the last. Frequent exhortations were given by the second chief to hurry along the tardy ones. Only males were scratched. Tobacco was distributed at this time among the occupants of the lodges by the town chief.

It has been customary in alternate years to do the scratching on the arm and breast, although both in 1904 and 1905 it was done on the arm.

The *yätcigī'* were constantly on the lookout for any man leaning against a post or tree. This is a forbidden indulgence, and they chastise every offender with their staffs. Anyone dropping off to sleep would be equally treated to a blow.

While the scarification was going on the two *ka'ká*, 'white man,' butchers, had barbecued the steer which was left on a scaffold at the rear of the west lodge behind the chiefs. (See diagram of square.) The meat was then distributed by the *ka'ka'* among the different families. With their long staffs they frequently went the rounds of the camp announcing to the women the progress of the rites, and seeing that they were preparing the food for the feast which was to follow the taking of the emetic. Consequently, the women were seen to bring to the border of the square, bowls of stewed meat, bread, boiled corn, coffee and other viands which were then picked up by the men and left on the scaffold with the carcass of the steer, until the ceremony of the emetic should be over. This handling of the food was a severe test to the hungry men. Sometimes it was necessary for the second chief to hurry up the bringing of the food by crying from the eastern edge of the square, whence all signals were given to the camp. The *yätcigī'* stood nearby ever ready to strike anyone found violating a taboo, with their poles. Dogs were frequently chased and belabored when in their roamings they crossed the edge of the square. Several men had to be treated to reminding blows by these young men as they forgot themselves and fell into a doze.

THE RITE OF THE EMETIC.

Now that the sun was about at the zenith and the medicines had been steeping in the sun long enough, it was time for the men to take the emetic in accordance with the instructions of the mythical Sun deity who declared that, as long as he rose from the east and beheld his people taking the sacred emetic, he would continue their tribal existence.

The first to take the emetic were the town chief and the three other square-ground Chiefs. (See Plate XV, 1.) They were followed by the four square-ground Warriors. Then four more Chiefs and four more Warriors took theirs. They dipped up the medicine with cups, two dipping from each pot. They always walked around the north side of the fire in approaching the pots. Nearly a quart was drunk by each individual.   After the first drink the men returned to their respective lodges of rank, and the four Chiefs led again for a second drink in the same order as before.   The town chief after this started toward the open space north of the square followed by the rest of the townsmen from the square, and there in the field copious quantities of the medicine were thrown up aided by fingers or weeds.   (See Plate XV, 2, also diagram of square.)

After a short interval, when all had taken their places in the square again, the emetic was taken by the four *yätcigī'* in the same manner as their predecessors.   When they had finished great relief was manifest throughout the camp, as the ordeal was practically over, and everything so far had gone on all right.

The second chief then led all the men in single file eastward toward the running water, where their paint was washed off and their hands also cleansed. The town chief, however, kept his place at the square, and on the forelog of the west arbor put four ears of green corn.   When the procession from the creek returned, all passed before these ears and rubbed their hands over them and then over their faces.   All then seated themselves in the proper lodges.   Some cobs of last year's corn were thrown in the fire as incense, the act symbolizing the passing out of use of the old crop.

Tobacco was then passed around and they smoked.   The town chief made a short speech relative to their fidelity, to the ritual and the successful termination of the ceremonies.   He invited them to take their fill of food and reminded them of the forgiveness due to petty offenders during the past season.   Hearty approbation was manifested toward his remarks.   When he took his seat and a few moments were passed in general deliberation, the food was distributed among those in the lodges and general feasting ensued.

The post at the southeast corner of the square was then taken down in attestation of the close of the taboo against aliens on the public square.

After eating, the next duty was to proceed to the nearest timber, where every man secured a branch of wood which he carried to a pile near the square. As he threw down his contribution, each gave a loud shout.   This wood was destined for consumption that night when the dances were to be performed. The duties of the ceremonial officers were now over.

Now that the ceremony was over for the time, the participants dispersed to their respective camps and enjoyed a period of social intercourse and rest. After some hours of rest a ball game was arranged by the elders for the young boys, for the purpose of giving them practice.   By the middle of the afternoon, sides were chosen among the young men for the more serious game, which was played for several hours.   Captains for the opposite sides were picked from among the best players.   A ceremonial sentiment underlaid the game, as no betting was indulged in this time.

By evening, when all had partaken of food and gotten a little rest, the fire was replenished and men and women assembled in the lodges as on the preceding night. The dancing was to continue all night, and a great number of the dances were to be celebrated. The general spirit of the gathering had then lost its severity and restraint. Laxity prevailed in every respect, together with some debauchery and licensed immorality which were treated with remarkable toleration by parents and elders.

DANCING.

On this, the second night, about six of the before-mentioned dances were performed. Although the general characteristics and functions of the dances have been described in the last chapter, a few of the peculiarities will be given again according to the actual cases as observed on both ceremonial occasions.

All of the Yuchi dances were this night performed around the fire in the center of the square. The movement was from right to left, contra-clockwise. The steps of the dancers were short, the motion being chiefly in the leg below the knee. In general effect the dance steps look more like shuffling. The foot, being brought down flat, gives forth a sound earning for the dance the name of Stamp, or Stump Dance, among the whites.

Male dancers held their arm nearest the fire, the left level, with their heads and the head slightly drooped, as they said, to protect their faces from the heat and glare of the fire. The true explanation of this is probably different, but is lost in obscurity. Women never assume this posture. Their arms were always at their sides when dancing, and their feet were never raised far from the ground. Motions were constantly made, as in the Buzzard dance when the arms of the performers were lowered and raised after the manner of a buzzard's wings.

On a tree at one side near the edge of the square a space of several feet of bark had been peeled off. Here a lot of red paint of mixed clay and grease had been smeared, and this was a source of supply for those who wished to daub themselves or renew their facial designs. Nearly all men wore the design of their society painted on their faces. Some were only promiscuously smeared with red and black.

In the nature of ornaments most of the men of the town wore white heron feather tremblers attached to their hats throughout the first few days. (Pl. VII, Figs. 7, 8.) These feathers, *gēhwané*, were shaved half-way up the quill to make them a little top heavy. The base is wound in the end of a wire spring about six inches long. The motions of the dancers impart a lively waving backward and forward to these feathers. As far as could be ascertained they were purely ornamental. Some dancers wore bunches of red, black, blue and white feathers in their hat bands. All wore their best clothes in the dances. The women, some of them, were decorated with a metal comb in the back of their hair, from which hung varicolored ribbons reaching nearly to the ground. In moving about, the wind carried these streamers out horizontally behind, producing a very pretty effect.

During the dances the town chief did not take part, but sat stolidly in his seat, in the west lodge, facing the square-ground and dancers. From time to time he gave a loud whoop or cry of encouragement and generally joined in the whoop at the end of the dance stanzas.

The dance songs were generally long, and divided into cantos. After each song or canto the leader whooped, the *goconé* echoed the cry and the dance circle broke up until the leader started the next canto. At the end of each song dancers imitated the cry of the animal named by the dance. The leader always knew the song and carried the air, the other dancer furnishing the chorus. Only the male dancers sang. Some of them carried fans of turkey buzzard or eagle tails. When a leader carried one of these fans he passed it to another man when he wished him to lead the next dance. A specimen of fan, made apparently of a buzzard's tail, is shown in Pl. VII, Fig. 9. The feather attach-

Fig. 41.   Feather Attachment of Wand.

ment is very simple, the quills being perforated and fastened side by side with a string of yarn strung through them transversely in two places.

A few of the dances observed during the ceremonies will now be described more in detail. Some of the song syllables were also obtained and are given in part. In such song burdens the part sung by the leader is given on the same line as that sung by the chorus of dancers, the two being separated by a space. Some of these dance songs were obtained from Laslie Cloud a Creek who claimed that both the Yuchi and the Creeks of his town, Taskigi, held them in common.

The Feather Dance, *łakané ctī*, until lately took place only at the ceremony of the Polecat settlement of the Yuchi. It was a daylight dance and occurred on the second day. It was performed before taking the emetic and again afterwards. The account of it was obtained from several informants.

There were four leaders, two abreast, the first two holding feather sticks, having six white heron's feathers attached to the end, one in each hand.

(See Pl. VII, Figs. 5, 6 and Fig. 41.) The next two shook hand rattles. The dancers formed in line two abreast and came running (dancing) sunwise toward a pile of earth, where the sweepings from the square were piled in a heap at the eastern side of the square sometimes to a height of three and one-half feet. Facing the sun they leaped over the pile as they reached it. Should any-one fail to make the leap or fall or drop anything while leaping he was seized by the four *yätcigī'* and taken to the creek where he was ducked before he could return to the square or pick up anything that he had dropped. The staffs of the *yätcigī'* were also decorated with white feathers for this dance.

This dance symbolized the journey of the sun over the square-ground the Sun deity was believed to be closely watching the dance from above. Should it not be properly enacted he was likely to stop in his course, according to the belief. The Feather Dance was known also as the Corn Dance.

The Gun Dance was called *Yät^{ε}ä' ctī*. This dance was said to be chiefly for pleasure, but it had some reference to the spirits dominating weapons and was believed to increase their effectiveness. It was performed at night by the Sand Creek town, and during the daytime by the Polecat settlement. The dancers held their firearms in the right hand. At the end of each song, (*a*), (*b*), (*c*), all were discharged toward the ground and the dancers whooped. The song is

> (*a*) *haigó didī wédidī,*   *yá^{ε}eya,*
> (repeated a number of times).
> (*b*) *helé helé maya,*   *gówena,*
> (repeated a number of times).
> (*c*) *waígeto wa^{ε}ayé,*   *héya,*
> (repeated a number of times).

The Duck Dance, *Cäné ctī*, was another in which it was sought to win the favor of the supernatural guardians of game. An element of thanks is said to have been recognized in these animal dances. The dancers held hands wind-ing around in circles and figures behind the leader, in single file. Men and women joined in promiscuously. The leader carried a hand rattle, and drum-ming also accompanied it. A band of visiting Shawnee joined in this dance with the Yuchi in 1904, arranging themselves so as to alternate in the file with Yuchi dancers. The songs were, in part,

> (*a*) *yē'ha yáléno,*   *wéhe yá^{ε}heya,*
> (repeated a number of times).
> *yagwē' hä'^{ε}*, a cry in imitation of the duck, given at end of
> the song; then *häñk, häñk, häñk* rapidly.
> (*b*) *wē'hē yáhēya,*   *áhēya wá^{ε}hēya,*
> (repeated a number of times).
> (Repeat cries as above.)

The Horse Dance, *Ba'tä' ctī*, had no unusual features. It was of the general type described. At the end of each song all the dancers grunted like stallions.

   (a) *yahó gʌni yá,*   *súnaga,*
         (repeated a number of times).
   yahó gʌni yá,
   (b) *yahówē ya,*   *yálēgē,*
         (repeated a number of times).
   (c) *hīyáyahó,*   *hē'lēna,*
         (repeated a number of times).

The dancers whinnied like stallions four times.

In the Buzzard Dance, *Yʌⁿtī' ctī*, the dancers waved their arms like the wings of a buzzard. At the end of each song all bent over, spat, and hissed like buzzards disgorging food. It was said to indicate bad breath and bad taste in the mouth. Sometimes the motion of the arms was slow, with the palms of hands turned down; sometimes it was fast, as in song (c). This was a totemic dance.

   (a) *yahólēha,*   *yagowē'ᵋē,*
         (repeated a number of times).
   (b) *tawaya,*   *hēlē',*
         (repeated a number of times).
   (c) *hánēwáyahē,*
         (repeated a number of times).
   (d) *sū'lī wáya hē,*
         (repeated a number of times).
   (e) *hē'ya yowē',*   *hʌnnē',*
         (repeated a number of times).
 nó haya,
         (arms raised high and slowly waved).

The Rabbit Dance, *Cadjwané ctī*, is another of the common type dances. The dancers held their left arm crooked between their faces and the fire. They began by squealing like rabbits. It was also a totemic dance.

   (a) *yohólena,*   *yohóᵋ oᵋ hʌ',*
         (repeated a number of times).
   (c) *wä háyo nä,*
         (repeated a number of times).
   (d) *yohólēna,*
         (repeated a number of times).
   (4) *wäháyonä',*
         (repeated a number of times).

The Fish Dance was called *Cūcpá ctī*, Pike Dance, or *Cudjᵋá ctī*, Catfish Dance. The dancers waved their arms at their sides like the fins of a fish.

Four whoops were given at the beginning. The Fish Dance was totemic also.
This dance was quite an important one. There was much more stamping and
shouting in it than in the others.

hóyalē hóyalē,	*yo–hū–ū–ho*[1],

      (shouted out and accompanied by stamping).

yē–hē–hō,	*yáleha*,

        (stamping, shouted).

yo–ū–ū–ho,

     (shouted, with violent stamping).

The Leaf Dance, *Yacá ctī*, was rather graceful in effect. The dancers
waved their hands imitating leaves blown by the wind. In this dance the
grateful shade of the summer foliage is recognized by the people as a blessing.
I was told that several women carried the hand rattle in the Leaf Dance. The
song was as follows and was sung four times with a great deal of repetition of
the different parts. The repetitions were very rapid and seemed quite irregular
toward the end.

wahī yonē',	*heya'*,

     (repeated a number of times).

*hēga*ᵋ *yonē'*,	*heya'*,

     (repeated a number of times).

hodjī' gä yó,

     (repeated a number of times).

The Shawnee Dance, *Yoⁿctá ctī*, is said to have been borrowed from the
neighboring Shawnee, with whom the Yuchi are very intimate. It is a very picturesque and animated dance, indeed, a general favorite. Only the drum is
used, one man beating it while several others sing. A line of women filed out
from one corner of the square holding hands, led by a Shawnee girl beautifully
dressed. Very soon the men from the different lodges came in between each
pair of women and took their hands. The whole line of alternating men and
women holding hands, then wound round and about the square-ground imitating
the movements of a serpent. The song syllables as remembered, consisted of *ya
na na we hé* repeated over and over. At intervals announced by a whoop the
dancers all faced right about and continued in that way until the next whoop.

The Buffalo Dance, *Wedīngá ctī*, was an important one. The dancers
held sticks in their hands. Formerly they wore buffalo robes on their backs and
the stuffed skins of the buffalo's head over their shoulders. The dancers held
their arms at their sides with the sticks clinched in their fists. Their bodies
were bent stiffly forward and they grunted like buffaloes. The first three

---

[1] The hyphen denotes emphasis and arrested voice.

songs only are given. First the leader sang a part, then the chorus, then all joined in the cry *yâ yâ īhō′*, or grunted.

>(a) *hē′ yalēna*, (repeated a number of times);
>   (grunting) *yâ yâ īhō′*.
>(b) *náwa yahá hēlē*,   *hēyō hówīya*,
>   (repeated a number of times).
>   *yâ yâ īhō′* (cry).
>(c) *hyó lena hyó lena hī′*,   *hyawá hēlē*,
>   (repeated a number of times).
>   *yâ yâ īhō′* (cry).

In the Chicken Dance, *Wētcᵋä′ctī*, the men and women held hands side by side, marching two abreast. Men were allowed liberties with the persons of their partners because they were imitating cocks. The singing in this appeared to be more in unison.

>(a) *yágowī hólē ha*,
>   *yahólēha yagowīᵋī′*,
>   (repeated a number of times).
>(b) *hégowī yahoya nalē hē gowīᵋī′*,
>   *yalē′hoya hánawīyeᵋé′*,
>   (repeated a number of times).
>(c) *hē′yahē nohē*,
>   *hē′nayanadawīya*,
>   (repeated a number of times).

In the Owl Dance, *Kyäⁿ′ctī*, there was the same form in dancing as in the Chicken Dance, but no liberties were allowed. In this each song was much repeated throughout. The accent was too varied to record.

>(a) *ahēyowana hä*.
>(b) *yowalē yowalēhē*.
>(c) *hayodjē haᵋ agē*.
>(d) *hayowana hayodjeᵋ haᵋagē*.
>(e) *tawayahēlē*.

The Crazy or Drunken Dance, *Tsebenbenēⁿ′ ctī*, was the last to be performed before daybreak of the second and last night of the ceremonies.

In character it was extremely obscene, as well as in words of the songs. The leaders frequently composed parts which they sang. They were given in these to ridiculing others. The commonest words seem to have been, "I am drunk; I want whiskey." The more selfrespecting women often refused to join in it, as temporary alliances were understood to result from intimacy between the sexes on this occasion. The men whinnied like stallions or mules as signals. The close of the last song was uproarious, being followed by general debauchery. Spectators were also sharers in the latter.

The whiskey, invoked in the words of the song, was considered a divine inflatus; the opinion of the Yuchi in regard to it seems to be analogous to the esteem in which the mescal or peyote is held among the western and southwestern tribes. There is, in fact, some reason to believe that the mescal worship may spread among the Yuchi if it continues eastward, as it has already gained a foothold among the conservative Pawnees and Osages.

The liberality of the Yuchi religious sentiment is seen in the manner in which dances have been invented for the worship of acculturated objects, like the cow, chicken, firearms, etc., which they did not know in early times. Constant borrowing has also taken place between the Yuchi and their neighbors, the Creeks, Shawnees and others. During the second night of the ceremonies visitors from other tribes were expected to perform some of their dances, which from all outward appearances belonged to the Yuchi ritual and were joined in by the Yuchi as well as by visitors. The *goconé* always extended the invitations to outsiders when their dances were desired.

THIRD DAY.—After the all-night dancing at the end of the second night, which was concluded by the Crazy or Drunken Dance, the townfolk disbanded. Those who lived at a distance went home to sleep and rest. Sometimes a few young people lingered about the square during these days, engaged in social intercourse or games.

FOURTH DAY.—The fourth day was spent at home in much the same way as the previous one.

FIFTH DAY.—On the fifth day the townsfolk assembled at the square again. as on the first day.

SIXTH DAY.—On the sixth day at noon another feast was prepared and eaten on the 'square. This meal consisted of meat.

The whole of the following night was given over to dancing and revelry like that of the second night.

SEVENTH DAY.—On the seventh day the ceremonial gathering was at an end, and all dispersed for the last time. The new year was now begun with a clean record, civilly and religiously, for the whole town. These continued days of assembly were held in 1905 with an unusual manifestation of interest, as the chiefs had decided not to hold the ceremonies another year.

At other times of the year dancing took place at gatherings, but they were regarded as entirely informal. Attendance on the part of the men was not compulsory at such times.

In concluding this account of the ceremonies of the Yuchi a few words might be said in the way of comparison with the rites and beliefs of surrounding culture areas.

The new fire rite, which was commonly found throughout the Southeast, has analogies in other regions. Nearly all occurrences of this kind, however, are found in the southern portion of the continent. A new fire rite was prominent in Mexico,[1] and among the Pueblo tribes of the Southwest.[2]

The idea of the town shrine also strongly suggests the sacred altars of the Southwestern tribes and the shrines or altars concerned in the ceremonies of the tribes of the Plains. In all of these altars from the Southwest, across the Plains to the Southeast a common element is to be found in the symbolic painting or color representations on the ground.

As regards the ceremonies of scarification and the taking of the emetic we again find a specialization, in the Southeast, of these features which are, however, widely distributed westward and southward. The scratching operation regarded as a form of torture has distant analogies among nearly all the tribes of the Plains, where the Sun Dance was performed. The emetic ceremony, found prominently in nearly every southeastern tribe, is also traceable across the Plains to the Southwest.[3] A difference is to be noted in the character of the public communal ceremonies as we go from east to west. In the Southeast every male in the town is a participant in them and must undergo every rite. On the Plains certain individuals only undergo the torture and the priests of the ceremony take the emetic. Again in the Southwest the ceremonies are performed characteristically by the priests, who alone take the emetic. There are besides a number of similarities in detail between the rites of the Plains, the Southeast and Southwest. Considering the matter as a whole, we are led, provisionally, to the opinion that, as regards ceremonials, a great deal of similarity characterizes the Southern area of North America extending in a sort of zone from the Atlantic along the Gulf and thence westward and southward to what may have been their center of distribution.

---

[1] The Mexican new fire ceremony at the beginning of each cycle is given in Die Culturvölker Alt-Amerikas, Dr. Gustav Brühl, New York, Cincinnati, St. Louis, 1875-87, pp. 237, 412.

[2] Cf. Fewkes, in American Anthropologist, N. S., Vol. 2, p. 138, for a discussion of the distribution of this rite.

[3] Cf. Dorsey, The Arapaho Sun Dance, Field Columbian Museum, Publication No. 75, Chicago, 1903; also The Cheyenne, same series, No. 103, p. 164, where dancers cause themselves to vomit near the end of the ceremony; also Dorsey, Mythology of the Wichita, Carnegie Institution, Wash., 1904, p. 16, where priests in ceremony take emetic. I was also informed that the Comanche cerebrated a rite before the season's first corn was eaten in which, during the performance of a round dance, all the villagers took an emetic brewed from a certain plant. See also Stevenson, The Sia Indians, Eleventh Report Bureau American Ethnology, 1894, p. 87; Voth, Oraibi Summer Snake Ceremony, Field Columbian Museum, Pub. No. 83, p. 347; Dorsey and Voth, Mishongnovi Ceremonies, same series, No. 66, pp. 159-261; Fewkes, Tusayan Snake and Flute Ceremonies, Nineteenth Report Bureau American Ethnology, 1900, p. 976.

TREATMENT OF DISEASE.

SHAMANISM.

Various practices are observed among the Yuchi for the cure of disease. They are chiefly songs used in conjunction with herbs, or other substances, without regard to their actual medicinal character, whether beneficial or harmful. In each settlement the town chief is one of the shamans who retains the knowledge of the plants and rituals. Among the Creeks the powers of shaman are open to any successful candidate, a remark which may apply to the Yuchi as well, though as far as could be learned only one such shaman lives in the Sand Creek settlement now and he is the town chief.

The treatment consists in giving the medicinal herbs to the patient, for internal or external application, and in performing other rites with appropriate songs of address to the supposed causes of the disorder.

The shamanistic rites of the Creeks and Yuchi are said to be identical. This has been observed in regard to the practices, and was asserted by informants from both tribes in regard to the songs and the medicinal herbs going with them. As information from the only Yuchi doctor in Sand Creek could not be had, a collection of songs in text and on the phonograph, a list of diseases with their causes, and the herb cures was made from a famous Creek shaman, *Kabítcimála*, Laslie Cloud, living near the Yuchi settlements.[1]

All bodily affliction is believed to come from the presence of some harmful foreign matter in the system, placed there either by some animal spirit or another conjurer. The origin is, however, mostly traceable to animals. As long as this substance remains in the body, health is impossible. Since trouble is likely to come from so many sources, the Yuchi finds it necessary to be constantly on guard against the operation of malignant spirits and conjurers by observing the taboos. Should a man unwittingly offend one of the animal spirits, he would suffer. The moment anyone feels pains or illness it is believed that some offence has thus been done. The first thing to do is to placate the spirit agency, and secondly to remove the material cause. The placation of the spirit is effected by some song or formula and the removal of the foreign matter is effected by the administration of some medicinal drinks. To have the obnoxious substance removed and the placation gone through with, the services of a shaman are required. The shaman must first discover the cause. This is done by secret methods, upon which his skill and reputation usually rest. Some shamans can diagnose by examining the sufferer's shirt, for which a charge of twenty-five cents or equivalent is made.

Certain roots and plants, steeped in water, are necessary aids to the shaman in driving out the trouble, and various formulae go with these medicines.

---

[1] See Memoirs of American Anthropological Association, Vol. 2, Part 2, The Creek Indians of Taskigi Town, p. 121.

The shaman secretes himself with the medicines, and filling a pot with water, steeps them, all the time blowing into the concoction through a hollow cane. This cane is about two and one-half feet long and has three red ribbons tied on it. (See Pl. VII, Fig. 1.) This takes place between the stanzas of the appropriate song. Nearly all of the songs are sung four times, then a long blowing is given the medicine, after which it is thought properly charged with magic power. It is then given to the patient, who drinks it and washes in it, applying it according to the shaman's advice. The song and ritual is believed to throw the disease into some animal, but not the one causing it. The following are a few of the medicine songs with the corresponding diseases, their symptoms and medicines.

Names of medicine songs, according to the creatures believed to cause the diseases.	Symptoms.	Medicinal Herbs.
Deer.	Swelling, boils	Cedar leaves.
Deer	} Headache	{ Willow species (?).
Sun.		{ Sunflower.
Young Deer	Swollen joints and muscles.	Cedar leaves and Deer Potato (*Licinaria scariosa*).
Water Moccasin	Swollen cheeks, toothache and sore gums.	Dried twigs and leaves.
Hog	Nausea and indigestion	(*Hierocicum* species).
Water Wolf	Nausea, dysentery	Sassafras.
Snake Hunting	Swollen face and limbs	Cedar leaves.
Little Turtle	Coughing, sores on limbs and neck.	Wild Cherry bark.
Panther	} Nausea, gripes	(?)
Wildcat		
Bear	Nausea, dysentery	(*Chenopodium* species).
Bird	Nausea, dysentery, stiff limbs.	Bird's nest.
Horse	Gastritis	Corn cobs.
Beaver	Pain in bowels, constipation.	Black Willow (?) and tulip (?).
Fish	Insomnia	Ginseng.
Great Horned Serpent.	Swollen limbs, lameness.	(?)
Raccoon	} Insomnia, Melancholia	(?)
Yellow Alligator		
Otter		
Ghost	Fever	(?)

The explanation of the origin of diseases and medicines, as given by my Creek informant, is as follows, in abstract, "Our ancestors of the olden time told it. The Deer said that he made the sickness and the medicine for it, thus (for the cure of trouble inflicted by him). The Bear . . . etc. The Many Snakes . . . etc. The Felines . . . etc. The Water Creatures . . . etc. The Seashore Creatures . . . etc."

Sickness is called *galen'*, 'trouble'. The expression for sickness is rather peculiar. There is no regular verb for it, so when a man is sick he says "Sickness, or trouble, feels me" (*galen' dzē yū'*).

Sympathetic healing appears to be the underlying theory in the use of the formulas and herbs. It characterizes the practices, so far as I know, of most of the southeastern tribes. A very conservative man named *Kyē'bané* is said to be the one best informed in shamanism, and it is likely that a collection of formulas could be obtained from him if he could be induced to part with his knowledge. Shamans hold their formulas in high esteem and will only impart them to chosen or favored persons, even then at monopoly rates of charge. If perchance ordinary persons come into possession of a knowledge of any formulas or remedies they make use of them the same as a regular shaman would. Spiritual appointment to the office does not seem to be entirely necessary for success. Anyone who knows some good cures can find employment in his neighborhood. Charges may be made for such treatment, but never need be paid until recovery or at least improvement is obtained.

To illustrate this I will give the experience of a Sand Creek Yuchi. He was quite clever in diagnosing and curing troubles among the Indians. Once while he was lounging about town with some friends, a very emaciated white man whom they knew passed by. He complained of being sick with some trouble which the physicians could not account for. The Yuchi casually remarked that he could cure him. Thereupon the white man declared that unless he could be cured he knew he would die, and that he would make it worth while to the doctor who cured him. The Yuchi became interested, secured the man's consent and started in with his shamanism. After working over the man for some weeks he began to improve and finally he was cured so that he could continue with his trade. The man did very well after this in health and in business but the Yuchi never asked him for pay. Some time afterwards the two met on the street in company with some friends. They remarked on the man's recovery and prosperity. He was very profuse in his praise of the Indian treatment and then to show his appreciation decided to be generous before the company. He munificently rewarded the expectant old shaman with the sum of fifty cents. This aroused a great deal of laughter among the Indians for some time after. The old man repeated it to everybody over and over again in lengthy terms, describing how he dug roots, sang songs and blew up medicine until he was breathless, for several months, to make a great case. But he never threatened to undo his cure.

I did not learn of the existence of any women who made a practice of shamanism.

The shamans furthermore possess secret means of divination. The town chief of the Sand Creek settlement gave an example of his power in this direction just before the annual celebration of 1904. I ventured to suggest to the master of ceremonies that I be allowed to fast in the square during the second day of the ceremony and take the emetic with the others. He told me that he would consult with the town chief about it to see whether I had eaten any corn or not, as, it will be recalled, those who have partaken of corn beforehand are forbidden the privilege of joining in the rites. In the meanwhile the town chief consulted a pot of medicine for the answer. Just what he did and how the answer appeared to him I could not learn. Shortly afterwards the master of ceremonies returned. I was told that the town chief found out that I had recently eaten corn and thereby violated the taboo. The master of ceremonies then asked me if it were true and I told him that it was.

One process of divination to learn the animal that causes disease is to conjure in some way over a pot of medicine until the image of the animal appears in the stuff. The shaman claims to see the reflection at the bottom of the pot. A similar process is common among the Creeks, and, incidentally, I learned that the Chickasaw seer divined by means of a piece of bear's dung or by the leaning of an upright pole.[1]

CEREMONIES.

What has so far been said in regard to the treatment of disease deals only with what might properly be called shamanism. Besides the regular practice of curing disease, which is in the hands of especially qualified persons, there are various methods employed by individuals for themselves when attacked by sickness or threatened with it. The town itself celebrates a public ceremony when threatened with evil in the shape of sickness, or when actually suffering from some epidemic. When a man becomes sick and does not desire to employ a shaman to cure him but prefers to treat himself, he can resort to the sweat-bath and emetic. In some respects the sweat-bath of the Yuchi is similar to that of many other American tribes, but there are some differences. A tent-like shelter is erected conveniently near running water and made thoroughly weather-tight. The operator then provides himself with a vessel of water, in which is steeped one of the several roots which acted as emetics. Tobacco, red root, or button snake root (the latter two having been mentioned

---

[1] See notes on Chickasaw Ethnology and Folk-Lore, Journal of American Folk-Lore, No. 76, p. 51 (1907).

in the account of the annual ceremonies) can be used for this. If tobacco be employed, only a palmful of the dried blossoms to a pail of water is necessary. Rocks are heated and piled in the center of the floor space in the tent, and when all is ready the patient enters naked, closes himself in and begins to drink as much of the emetic as he can. When two or three dipperfuls have been swallowed vomiting begins. The operator vomits upon the hot rocks and the liquid turns immediately into a cloud of steam. In this way the process of drinking and vomiting on the hot rocks is kept up until the man is thoroughly sweated and purged internally. Then he emerges and plunges into the river.

The sweat-bath is taken not only when sickness is felt but from time to time by different individuals to ward it off. It is done also to right one's self with the Sun deity, and before serious undertakings like the hunt, the journey or the warpath. The town also has a general public ceremony, the object of which is to ward off not only sickness but evils of other sorts whatever they might be. The ceremony embodies the ideas of physical purging, of purification in a religious sense and of propitiation to the various supernatural beings. It consists of dancing and vomiting.

The ceremony is called *Tsotĭ'benēⁿ*, 'Medicine Drinking.' When sickness, or trouble in general is abroad or threatens the town, the town chief called the families to the square-ground for the observance. At sundown they gather while a quantity of the emetic is prepared. Everyone is given to drink until he vomits. Then in the interval the proper persons prepare more of the draught, while the people spend the time in dancing various dances. When the medicine is ready again the *goconē'*, the leader of the Warrior society, calls the people for another drink. This they take, allowing it to have its effect, then fall to dancing again. During the whole ceremony, which is carried on all night, no one is allowed to sleep or doze. The officers of the Warrior society have to see to it that no one breaks this rule. The dancing and drinking are continued until sunrise, at which time the ceremony is ended.

A few other individual practices for curing sickness in children were observed. These are, so to speak, family methods quite generally known and practiced without any particular ceremony. For a sore mouth and irritation of the intestines the fresh blood of a chicken is thought to be effective. The living fowl is cut through the back of the neck, the bleeding stump thrust into the open mouth of the sufferer, and the blood swallowed as it flows. For whooping cough the sufferer drinks some water in which a crow was soaked whole. The analogy is said to be drawn between the coughing and the crow's cawing.

Incidentally it was learned that the Indians when suffering with toothache never try to extract the tooth but, if they do anything, just chew some strong herbs, sometimes tobacco.

I found a man with a piece of some small whitish root, which looked as though it might be ginseng, in his money bag. He said that it was good to keep away sickness. He also used an infusion of it to relieve his child of croup at night. He said that he always carried it when traveling.

Tobacco blossoms are employed as an ordinary physic and emetic. Three or four of the dried blossoms suffice when steeped in a medium sized pot of water.

The common method of treating nose-bleed is to pour cold water over the sufferer's head.

AMULETS.

Protective amulets were more commonly worn heretofore than now. One specimen was obtained from the neck of a child. Its particular function was to bring sleep and rest to the wearer. The thing consists of an insect larva sewed tightly in a buckskin covering decorated on one side with blue and white beads (Fig. 42). The fetish symbolizes a turtle, the similarity in form being carried out further by three little loops of white beads representing the hind legs and tail. A double potency was ascribed to this object since it embodies the influence of two creatures who spend much of their existence in a dormant state. In the figure white beads are represented by open spaces and dark blue beads by the filled-in spaces. The center row of lighter blue is shown by the shaded spaces.

Fig. 42. Amulet.

Another charm to keep children from getting sick was composed of some small white bones wrapped up in buckskin or rag and tied to their necks or hammocks. Bones of this sort were also believed to prevent children from crying in the night and to protect them in general from the effects of all possible evil. It is also understood that men wore small, curiously formed objects, or trophies, which had some relation to events in their career, in the belief that the things would prove effectual in protecting and guiding them in some way.

MYTHOLOGY.

Some of the most important mythologic accounts have been given in the description of religious beliefs and need not be repeated . If the following interpretation of Southern mythology be correct, it would seem that the myths of the Yuchi and the other southeastern tribes belong in one fairly homogeneous group, and that the fundamental myth elements, here somewhat specialized on account of local interests, also belong in the extensive common category widely distributed over the continent.

The cosmogonic idea of the Yuchi, and the other tribes of the Southeast, is purely creational, in contrast to the transformational concept of the Algonkian, Siouan, and especially of the tribes of the northwest Pacific coast. The cosmogonic myth type of the Cherokee, Muskogi and Yuchi is, with a few exceptions, as follows:

Water is everywhere. The only living creatures are flying beings and water beings. They dispute over existing conditions and some decide to make, a world. They induce Crawfish (Creek, Yuchi) or Beetle (Cherokee) to dive for it. When earth is brought up from the depths of the water, it is made to grow until it becomes the present earth. Buzzard is deputed to fly over, and flatten it, but he tires and so causes roughness in the form of mountains. After this comes the creation of sun, moon and stars for the benefit of the terrestrial creatures. Then follows the creation of man, which varies too much among the types for composite rendering.[1]

The following two classes may be distinguished in the myths: the sacred, relating to the culture hero and the deeds of the animal creators, and the commonplace, relating to the Rabbit trickster, various animals, and their exploits, etc. The latter class, subject to much variation and change at the hands of different individuals, is extremely characteristic of the whole Southeast.

The culture hero concept so general throughout America is found among the Yuchi embodied in the personality of the Sun. The trickster and transformer character is found in the Rabbit, a personage here quite separate and distinct from the culture hero.

The culture hero concept is closely connected with religion and ritual, while the trickster concept is not. The culture hero is believed to be the author of Yuchi tribal existence, their clan system, ceremonies, etc., but does not

---

[1] Myths of the Creeks, W. O. Tuggle, MSS. Bur. Amer. Eth.; Myths of Cherokee, J. Mooney, Nineteenth Rep. Bur. Amer. Eth., p. 239; Creek Inds. of Taskigi Town, Speck, op. cit., p. 145.

seem to be concerned in the creation myth.   As the myth relates, the Sun deity placed the Yuchi under obligation to follow out his instructions in worship to insure their tribal integrity and they look to him as the author of all good.

The culture hero myth of the Yuchi, with the one personality, his coming, his creation of the Yuchi, his instructions to them, and his departure and promise, suggests a legend of the Creeks quoted by numerous authors and first recorded by Hawkins.[1]   Here four deities, 'hiyouyulgee',[2] probably cardinal point deities, appear analogous to the Sun deity of the Yuchi.   Although no other authentic mention has been made of the entire myth among the Creeks, the one described by Hawkins looks very much like a partial outline of the Yuchi culture-hero myth.

Another important mention of the four culture heroes of the Creeks and the origin of ceremonies and medicine plants is found in the Tuggle collection of Creek Myths.[3]   The myth comes from Tookabatchie (*Tukabaχtci*) town.

Four persons came from "Esakutumisi"[4] and brought some metal plates to them, which are retained and exhibited to this day in the public square at the ceremonies, as town "palladia."   These four deities instructed the Tookabatchie, prophesied the coming of the whites, bequeathed them their ceremonial care of the metal plates and made their future welfare dependent upon it. One of the four died and over the spot where he was buried a plant appeared which was tobacco.   (Tookabatchie town is credited by Tuggle with a migration legend similar to that of Kasiχta.)

Owing to the fact that so many of the myths, or parts of myths, current among the southeastern tribes are analogous to those found among the southern negroes, much discussion has arisen over their origin.   Without regard to the names of characters involved in the tales, the elements of action ought to be the means of determining to some extent the source of a large number.   Where analogous events are found in the mythologies of other American tribes less

[1] Myth from Hawkins,   Sketch of Creek Country, 1798–99, pp. 81, 82.
"Opinion of Tassekiah Micco on Origin of the Creeks, and the New Fire.
"There are in the forks of Red river . . . . . . .two mounds of earth.   . . . . .Here they were visited by the Hiyouyulgee, four men who came from the four corners of the world.   One of these asked the Indians where they would have their fire.   They pointed to a place; it was made, and they sat down around it.   The Hiyouyulgee directed that they should pay particular attention to the fire, that it would preserve them and let Esaugetuh Emissee know their wants.   One of these visitors took them and showed them the passau (Button Snake Root, *f³âde'*, of the Yuchi); another showed them the Micco ho yo ejau (Red Root, *to tcala'*, of the Yuchi), then the Auchenau (Cedar) and Tooloh (Sweet Bay) . . . .   After this, the four visitors disappeared in a cloud going from whence they came . . . ."
[2] Ha'yayΛ'lgi, ' Light people,' 'People of the light,' Brinton, Myths of New World, pp. 94, 95.
[3] MS. unpublished in Bureau American Ethnology.
[4] Hisákida imíssi, 'Master of Breath.'

influenced by outsiders, it may be safely assumed that those myths, or parts, are native to America.   And in some cases, too, purely indigenous myth actions have been recorded from both Africa and America.   No discussion is necessary in such cases of accidental similarity.   But a large number of Indian myths of the Southeast show both Indian and negro aspects, and it is in regard to this class of myth that the question arises.

From Indian informants it has been recently learned that stories describing the cunning and wisdom of various animals corresponding to clan totems, have been welcomed by the Indians to illustrate the superiority of some particular totemic animal.   As the honor of the totem is carefully maintained by each clan, it is quite natural that any tale adding to the glory of a totem should be adopted by the members of the clan and told as though it were actually concerned with their totem.   Wherefore elements of African or European myths have been continually engrafted in whole or in part on the native stock of animal tales, until it is hardly possible now to distinguish which is which.   This explanation was furnished by Indians and seems to be generally understood among the Yuchi, Creek and Chickasaw, and it may possibly apply to other southern tribes in a like manner.

As the Yuchi material appears to belong so inseparably to the general type of mythology of the Southeast as a whole, we shall deal in brief with the whole region instead of with the Yuchi alone.   Such a thing as exclusively pure Yuchi mythology, I fear, could not truthfully be spoken of nowadays, since borrowing has gone on so extensively.   A few cognates of the myths, found by collateral reading in the mythologies of other tribes, are given incidentally in footnotes.   They do not represent any attempt to make a complete concordance.

Leaving the important myths relating to cosmogony, we find a great many myths relating to heroes, monsters, tricksters and other beings concerned with transformation in the Southeast, some elements of which are cognate with Algonkian and Iroquois myths, others with those of the Southwest.   A general review of these myths from the Southeast brings out the following features and comparisons.

Stories of monsters clad in bone, stone, metal or scales are very characteristic of the region.   The monster is usually a cannibal, and is finally slain by persons or beings who have learned the secret of its only vulnerable spot.   The culture hero often appears as the slayer.[1]   The account of the trickster who,

[1] Creek (Migration Leg. of Creeks, Gatschet, p. 248). Cherokee (Cher. Myths, Mooney, 19th Rep. Bur. Amer. Eth., pp. 319, 326, 311). Menomini (Menomini Inds., Hoffman, 14th Rep. Bur. Am. Eth., p. 229). Micmac (Alg. Leg. of N. E., Leland, p. 38). Wyandot (Wyandot Folk-Lore, Connelly, p. 91). Sarcee (J. A. F. L., Journal of American Folk-Lore. Vol. XVII, p. 181). Saulteaux and Cree (Alg. Ind. Tales, E. R. Young, p. 166). Dakota (Contr. to N. A. Ethn., Vol. IX, p. 101). Sia (11th Rep. Bur. Amer. Eth., Stevenson, p, 45). Jicarilla Apache (Amer. Anth., Vol. XI, p. 208). Wichita.

when invited to dine with a friend who produces food by miracles, is unable to imitate his host when he himself tries, is even more general and uniform.[2] Other elements of wide distribution are: The race between two rivals and the victory of the trickster by strategy.[3] The narrative of the men who travel to the spirit land to visit some deity for the purpose of obtaining a boon, upon the receipt of which one of them fails to heed certain restrictions, and suffers disastrous results.[4] The accepted type of what is now known as the magic flight or obstacle myth, with various modifications.[5] The stealing of fire by the culture hero, or an animal concourse (Cherokee), or Rabbit (Creek, Yuchi).[6] The dispute over day and night by the animals, and the introduction of day.[7] And lastly, for the present, the tar-man story, so common throughout western Africa and among the American negroes,[8] which tells of the capture of a rogue by setting a figure made of adhesive pitch, or other substances, where he must come into contact with it. The Jicarilla Apache version, though remote from the Southeast, is closely analogous to

[2] Creek (Tuggle, MS.). Cherokee (Mooney, p. 273). Thompson River (Teit, p. 40). Algonkin (Leland, p. 208–213). Jicarilla Apache (Russel, J. A. F. L., Vol. II, p. 265–66). Arapaho (Field Col. Mus., Vol. V, p. 116). Navaho (Mathews, p. 87). Micmac (Rand, p. 302-3). Chilcotin (Trad. of the Chilcotin, Farrand, p. 18). Biloxi (J. A. F. L., Vol. VI, p. 49). Wichita.

[3] Creek (Tuggle, MS.). Cherokee (Mooney, pp. 270, 290). Menomini, Saulteaux and Cree (Young, p. 246). Zuni (Cushing, Zuni Folk-Tales, p. 277). Arikara (Trad. of the Arikara, Dorsey, p. 143). Wichita.

[4] Creek, Cherokee (Mooney, p. 253–5). Menomini (Hoffman, p. 118). Thompson River (Teit, pp. 53, 85). Algonkin (Leland, p. 94). Saulteaux and Cree (Young, p. 244). Micmac (Rand, p. 233). Article in Amer. Anth., Dorsey, Vol. VI, p. 64. Omaha (Cont. to N. A. Eth., Vol. VI. p. 185–188). Shawnee (Gregg, Commerce of Prairies, Vol. II, p. 239–240). New Brunswick (Parkman, Jesuits in N. A.). Chinook, Wichita.

[5] Creek (Tuggle, MS.). Menomini (Hoffman, p. 188–9). Thompson River (Teit, p. 92). Passamaquoddy (Leland, p. 214). Navaho (Mathews, p. 102). Dakota (Riggs, p. 108, Vol. IX). General European distribution (Boas, J. A. F. L., Vol. 4, 1891, p. 19). Cree (Canadian Sav. Folk, MacLean, p. 71). Blackfoot (J. A. F. L., Vol. VI, p. 44). Mohegan (J. A. F. L., Vol. XVI, p. 104). Cheyenne (J. A. F. L., Vol. XVI, p. 108). Chippewyan (J. A. F. L., Vol. XVI, p. 80–84). Ojibway (Schoolcraft, Myth of Hiawatha, p. 249). Wichita.

[6] Creek (Tuggle, MS.). Jicarilla (Russel, p. 261). Cherokee (Mooney, p. 240). Menomini (Hoffman, p. 126). Saulteaux and Cree (Young, 96–105, 89–94). Nez Percés (J. A. F. L., Vol. 4, p. 327). Chilcotin (Memoirs Amer. Mus. Natl. Hist., Vol. IV). Tsimshian (Tsimshian Texts, Boas, p. 31). Maidu (Bull. Amer. Mus. Natl. Hist., Vol. XVII, Part II, p. 65).

[7] Cherokee (Mooney, p. 251). Thompson River (Teit, p. 61). Iroquois (Second Rep. Bur. Am. Eth., Smith).

[8] Africa (Ewe Speaking People, Ellis, p. 275; Yoruba Speaking People, Ellis, p. 252). Amer. Negro (Uncle Remus, Harris, p. 23). Angola (Chatelain, p. 183–9). Kaffir (Theal., p. 179). Louisiana (J. A. F. L. Memoirs, Vol. II, Fortier, p. 98). Bahama (J. A. F. L. Memoirs, Vol. III, Edwards, p. 73).

the latter account. In eastern Algonkian, Gluscap punishes a rogue, Pitcher, by causing him to stick to a tree by his back, and transforming him into a toad. Arapaho tradition tells of a child, born from the cut in a man's foot, being pursued by a buffalo who wants to marry her. She takes refuge in a hollow stump to which the buffalo sticks, when he strikes it with his head in trying to dislodge her. In Wichita, After-birth Boy and his brother lay on a stone which they find, and stick to it.[9]

There are a few more legends that deserve emphasizing in their connection with the Southeast. One of these is the migration legend, found in all branches of the Muskogi, the Yuchi and the Cherokee. Nearly all the Algonkian tribes have it, and the Plains tribes share it.[10]

The common element to the whole region is the eastward or westward journey of the soul and the obstacles it meets with. The most general type of obstacle is the cloud swaying at the end of the earth, where it and sky meet. This is the barrier to the spirit world, through which everyone desiring entrance to the spirit realm must pass.[11] Some of the transformations brought about by the animal creators of the Southeast are the procuring of land,[12] fire,[13] tobacco[14] and the bestowing of characteristics upon various beasts.

Lastly, mention need only be made of the almost universal occurrence, in North America, of the tradition which recounts the experiences of someone who fell into a trance, believed that he passed over to the spirit world where he saw the supreme deity, received a message from him to the people on earth and eventually returned to life, becoming a sort of prophet or messenger of the supreme deity. The myth explaining the origin of death, wherein death is introduced upon the earth through the mistake or disobedience of someone, or by mere chance, is also fairly typical of America.

---

[9] Creek (Tuggle, MS.). Cherokee (Mooney, p. 271–2). Jicarilla Apache (Russel, J. A. F. L., Vol. II, p. 268). Algonkin (Leland, p. 48). Arapaho (Pub. of Field Col. Museum, Vol. V, p. 153). Wichita (J. A. F. L., Vol. XVII, p. 159). Biloxi (J. A. F. L., Vol. VI, p. 48). Osage (Traditions of the Osage, G. A. Dorsey, p. 24).

[10] Cherokee (Mooney, p. 391). Creek (Migration Legend, Gatschet). Choctaw, Chicasaw, Hitchiti (Gallatin, Synopsis of Ind. Tribes, Amer. Antiq. Soc., Vol. II, p. 100, 1836). Lenape (Brinton, The Lenape and their Legends, p. 138, 141-3). Tonkawa (Mooney, Harper's Mag., Aug., 1901). Kiowa (17th Rep. Bur. Amer. Eth., Part 1, p. 153). Sarcee (J. A. F. L., Vol. XVII, p. 180). Tuscarora (Legends of Iroquois, Elias Johnson, p. 43). Menomini (Hoffman, p. 217). Blackfoot (Amer. Anth., Vol. 5, p. 162). Nanticoke (Lenape and their Legends, p. 139). Shawnee (Gregg, Commerce of the Prairies, Vol. II, p. 256). Arikara (Trad. of Arikara, Dorsey, p. 31).

[11] Cherokee (Mooney, p. 255–6). Micmac (Rand, p. 233). Siouan (Amer. Anth., Vol. VI, p. 64, Dorsey). Iroquois (Amer. Anth., 1892, p. 344). Shawnee (Gregg, Commerce of Prairies, Vol. II, p. 239–40). New Brunswick (Parkman, Jesuits of N. A.). Thompson River (Teit, p. 85, 53). Menomini (Hoffman, p. 206). Tillamook (Boas, J. A. F. L., Vol. II, p. 30). Ottawa (Schoolcraft, p. 386). Wichita.

[12] Cherokee, Creek, Yuchi.   [13] Creek, Yuchi, Cherokee Myths, p. 200.   [14] Ibid., p. 254.

SUPPLEMENTARY MYTHS.

5. Origin of the Other Tribes, and a Chief's Visit to Receive the Creator's Prophecy.

Now the people had come upon the earth. The Shawnee came from above. The Creeks came from the ground. The Choctaw came from the water. The Yuchi came from the sun.

So *Gohäntoné* appointed a day for them to meet and mingle, because he thought at first that it would be better for them to do that. Accordingly they met at the place of sunrise, in the east, and mingled together in friendship. They smoked together and held a council. After considering, they concluded that it would be better for all if they did not mix up. And henceforth they separated, each tribe going its own way and living alone.

The Shawnee said, "Our name is Shawnee, and we'll go off by ourselves." So they went.

The Creeks said, "We are Muskogi, and we'll go off by ourselves."

The Choctaw said, "We're Choctaw." And they went away.

The Yuchi were there too, and they said, "Our name is Yuchi." And they in turn left. Each tribe selected its own place to live in, and went there.

Now after a while, when they had been separated some time, *Gohäntoné* thought the thing over and said,

"You have nothing. So I'll give you something. I'll give you all the earth."

Then he gave them the earth, and they scattered over it.

Now after a while *Gohäntoné* thought the matter over again. Then a Creek chief died. When the chief was dead he appeared before *Gohäntoné*, who said to him,

"This land belongs to you and your children forever. This land will be yours forever, but these whites who have just come will overwhelm you and inherit your land. They will increase and the Indian will decrease and at last die out. Then only white people will remain. But there will be terrible times."

So spoke *Gohäntoné* to the dead Creek chief. For four days he lay dead, then he came to life again. When he woke up he was well. He immediately called a great council. Shawnee, Choctaw, Creeks and Yuchi all assembled to hear him, and he told them all that he had seen and heard. He told them that the land would belong to the Indian forever, but the white man would overrun it. So the thing is coming to pass as *Gohäntoné* said.

6. Rabbit Steals Fire for the People.

In the beginning there was no fire on the earth, and there seemed to be no way to get it. Therefore, when the people wanted to eat flesh, they had to eat it raw. Finally the Rabbit said that he knew where fire was, and even said that he could get it. Then the people went into camp and took council. They decided to send Rabbit to get the fire that he spoke of.

"If you know where fire is, then go and get it," they said to him.

So Rabbit started out, and swam across the ocean, because he knew that fire was only to be had on the other side of the sea. The people over there were having an olden time dance, and when Rabbit appeared among them they said,

"Here is a man who belongs on the other side of the sea. So watch him well."

They selected four of their number to watch him. Now because Rabbit was such a good dancer, they soon chose him to lead them in one dance after another. So while he was leading they urged the four guardians of Rabbit to watch him very closely.

Now when Rabbit began to lead, he took a large shawl and wrapped it about his head and wound a number of berry leaves into it until the whole was very large. Then they danced very hard. But suddenly Rabbit picked up a coal from the fire and put it on his head among the berry leaves and ran away toward his own land. All the people started after him, but they could not catch him. He got safely over the sea with the burning coal, and was crossing a prairie near home when he dropped the coal, and the timber all about was set on fire. All the woods got on fire. The people ran out and secured the burning sticks and gave them to each family, so that they all could have fire. And it was never allowed to go out.

7. Rabbit Obtains Fire. (Second Version. Abstract.)

The Rabbit went across the ocean for fire and got in among people who were dancing. They were the people who possessed fire. He took some of the fire in his hand and jumping into the ocean swam across with it. When he had landed it began to rain, then he put the fire in a stump. When this took fire he scattered the burning pieces all around and the woods caught fire. From this the Indians got it.

8. Four Men Visit the Spirit Land to Recover Their Wives, and Death Originates.

Four Yuchi who had wives decided one day to kill them. So they killed the four women. "There is no such thing as death. So let us go and hunt them," said they.[1]

---

[1] The implication in this statement is that death was then non-existent.

Accordingly the four husbands set out to find their wives. They said, "Let us go where the Creator is." They set out westward and traveled a long while, coming at length to a place where there was a great cave. Before its mouth swayed a great cloud, in such a manner that they could not get by it or around it, for it was moving up and down. They saw that their journey would end here unless they could devise some means of passing the cloud. It was decided that they imitate something very swift and get in in that way. Said one of the men, "I'll be a deer." So he became a deer, and when the cloud raised up the next time, he jumped in. The next said, "I'll be a panther." And when the cloud raised up, he jumped in. The third man said, "I'll be a bear." And the next time the cloud raised up, he too jumped in. They had all jumped at the right time, and had succeeded. Now the fourth man said, "I am a man, and I'll be a man." And when he tried to get in, the cloud fell on his head and crushed him.

Then the three men who had reached the inside of the cave took their natural shape as men, and began to climb up the back of the cloud within the cave. After they had been some time climbing, they came to a wonderful scene, and as they went on they beheld an old woman seated there. The old woman was the sun. When she saw them she spoke to them.

"My sons, are you come. Are you not hungry?"

And the men said that they were hungry. Accordingly she planted a hill of corn, a hill of beans, and a hill of squash for each man. Now when they saw her doing this, they thought, "Well, as we are so hungry shall we have to wait for these things to grow before we can eat?" But the old woman knew their thoughts, and replied as though they had spoken out loud. She said,

"You think you won't eat very soon, but you won't have long to wait."

Even then the plants began to sprout and grow up, and soon they fruited, and it was not long before they gathered the corn, beans and squashes, and were ready to eat. The old woman then put a small quantity of the vegetables before each man. But they said, "Do you think that that little will fill us?" In reply, she said to them, "There will be some left over."

When they had finished eating, it was as she had said. There was some left over. Now the old woman spoke to the men again.

"What did you come here for? What do you want?" she asked them.

"We had four wives who are dead. We lost them, and they told us to hunt for them. So we are here."

"Well, they are here," said the old woman, "we are going to have an all-night dance, and the women will be there. Then you will see them."

Now the men were deciding whether to stay for the dance, or to go on. And while they were thinking over it, a panther monster came up, and they were very much afraid. But as soon as they saw him, the old woman lifted up her dress and told the men to come and get beneath it; they went under and she protected them. When the great monster came near, he said to her, "I smell people." But the old woman said, "You smell me." The monster was deceived and went away. Then when it became time the men went to the dance. They arrived at the place where they were dancing, and the men could hear the dance but they couldn't see anything. They said to the old woman,

"We can hear, but we cannot see. So give us a sign so that we may know that our wives are here."

Then the old woman got a coal from the fire and put it on the hip of one of the women who was now dancing with the rest. She did the same with each woman until the four had coals of fire on their hips. Now all that the men could see was the coal, when the women were dancing. But they stayed there watching. Soon the old woman said to them,

"If you cannot see, lay down and go to sleep."

So they did as they were told, and went to sleep. The old woman left them, and getting four large gourds, made holes in them and put one woman in each gourd. Then she carried the gourds to where the men were, and woke them up, saying, "Here are your women." She laid the gourds down, one near each man, and said,

"Now lie down and sleep again. When you wake up you will be back on earth. But when you wake up, don't open the gourds." She told them, "When you get back to your people, go to a dance and take these gourds with you."

Then they went to sleep again, and after a while woke up. They were back on the earth. They went on until they reached their people. But on the way, one of the men became impatient, and opened his gourd. Immediately a great wind came out and went up in the air. So the other three kept theirs and didn't open them. At last they reached their own land. When the time for a dance came around they took their gourds with them. While they were dancing they hit their gourds on the ground and broke them. The women jumped out and joined them in the dance. But the man who broke his beforehand, when he saw the other women restored to their men, wept. Now that's the way it was done.

The three who had done as the old woman told them, had a good time and were afterwards called by the others, "the people hunters." They were considered to be very wise, and in a short time they all became great chiefs and councillors in their tribe.

9. Tobacco Originates from Semen.

A man and a woman went into the woods. The man had intercourse with the woman and the semen fell upon the ground. From that time they separated, each going his own way. But after a while the woman passed near the place again, and thinking to revisit the spot, went there and beheld some strange weeds growing upon it. She watched them a long while. Soon she met the man who had been with her, and said to him, "Let us go to the place and I will show you something beautiful." They went there and saw it. She asked him what name to call the weeds, and he asked her what name she would give them. But neither of them would give a name. Now the woman had a fatherless boy, and she went and told the boy that she had something beautiful. She said, "Let us go and see it."

When they arrived at the place she said to him, "This is the thing that I was telling you about." And the boy at once began to examine it. After a little while he said, "I'm going to name this." Then he named it, 'ī', 'tobacco.' He pulled up some of the weeds and carried them home carefully and planted them in a selected place. He nursed the plants and they grew and became ripe. Now they had a good odor and the boy began to chew the leaves. He found them very good, and in order to preserve the plants he saved the seeds when they were ripe. He showed the rest of the people how to use the tobacco, and from the seeds which he preserved, all got plants and raised the tobacco for themselves.

10. Wind Seeks His Lost Sons and Kills the Iron Monster.

The Wind came out of the east and was lying somewhere, they say. He had four young men; they were his sons. One of them once said, "Let us go and look at the earth." That's why they went, and they haven't come back yet. So the young man went west and was gone a long time; he has never come back. Soon after, the second young man went and did not come back. Then the third young man went and he did not come back. None of them came back.

Now the Wind said, "I will go myself." He prepared and got everything ready. He told them to bring him a chair. They brought him a large terrapin. Then he ordered his pipe, telling them to bring him a bullfrog. Then he called for his pipe-stem. They brought a kind of snake and made a pipe-stem. He told them to get his tobacco. They brought him snake dung for tobacco. He told them to get his ammunition bag. They got him another snake for the ammunition bag. And when he told them to bring a belt for the ammunition bag, they brought him a bullsnake's hide for that. Then the Wind was ready.

He got up and started toward the west, the way the young men had gone before him. He followed their trail, traveling a long while, and at last came to a creek. Across the creek on the opposite bank he saw a white rooster. A short distance back there was a house. Now when the rooster saw him it flew over and alighted on the roof of the house. Then someone came out and crossed the creek in a little boat to meet him. Then the man in the boat told Wind to get in with him and go across. But Wind said that he had his own way to get across. So he put the terrapin in the creek and got on his back and the terrapin carried him across. Then they went on and soon reached the house. When Wind got to the house, the man gave him a chair and told him to sit down. Wind said that he had his own chair. He took the terrapin and sat down on him. The man then asked Wind to smoke with him. Wind said that he was willing, but that he had his own tobacco. And taking the snake dung, he put it in the frog's mouth, filling it up.

"Now all that I need is a little fire to light my tobacco with," said Wind. But he had his own fire. Taking the joint snake he had with him he struck a fire, and soon had a light for his pipe. He lighted it in that way. Then taking the other snake which was the pipe-stem, he inserted this in the frog's anus. So the pipe was finished, and in that way Wind could smoke with his host.

Now the owner of the house was a bad man; a man who could not be killed. He was made of iron. So he was Iron Man. Wind knew all about that, and he even knew that Iron Man had killed his four young men. Then Wind decided to kill him. When he smoked, he drew in a great deal of smoke and blew it on Iron Man. And that is the way he killed him. When Iron Man was dead, his wife came up and said to Wind,

"You killed my man. Let's marry."

But Wind said that he would not. He asked her where his four young men were and what had become of them. Then she told him all about them. She told him to go where he would find a certain dead tree near the water. She told him that if he would go and cut this tree down and throw it in the water, the four young men would come up from it. Then she guided Wind to the tree and said to him, "Cut it down." She got an axe and Wind cut the tree down. Then he threw it in the water as Iron Man's wife had told him. And the four young men came out of the water. When they stood on the ground they all looked black. They recognized Wind, but they told him that they were not under his control any longer. "Well, I'll make something different out of you, then," he said to them. Then one of the young men said, "What shall I be?" But Wind did not answer him, for that.

"I'll be a wolf," said the second. So the Wind told him to go into the woods, and he went.

Wind asked the third what he would be. "I'll be a crow," said he. Then Wind asked the fourth what he would be. "I'll be a raven," said the fourth young man. Wind told him to go into the forest. Now the first young man who had spoken too soon was the only one left. And Wind said to him, "What will you be?" "I'll be a dog," said he. "Well, you go and stay with the wolf," said Wind to him. And he went.

Now Wind was through with the young men. He said, "Some day I will go back where I came from. As I go I'll leave nothing in my way."

Wind has never come back; he is there yet. But some day he will come. That is what the old Yuchi say.

11. The Lost Yuchi.

They say the Yuchi all lived together in the old days. They had a dance, and while they were dancing, a quarrel arose among them. Some of them had bear hides upon their backs, and the rest were dancing with wildcat skins. The people who wore the bear hides then departed. They went west, over the great mountains. The others who had the wildcat skins remained. All the Yuchi here are the wildcat hide people. But what became of the bear hide people no one knows. They are both Yuchi but they cannot find each other.

12. Origin of Thunder and Lightning.

There is a great being, whose name is *Koⁿsánoⁿwī*. He rides over the seas upon a great blacksnake. When he goes in and out of the water, there is a great noise. That is the thunder. Sometimes the great snake shakes his tail, and that is what makes the lightning. But that is another story.

13. Why the Cedar Tree is Red-Grained[1], and How the Sun Was Rescued from a Sorcerer.

An unknown mysterious being once came down upon the earth and met people there, who were the ancestors of the Yuchi Indians. To them this being taught many of the arts of life, and in matters of religion admonished them to call the sun their mother as a matter of worship. Every morning the sun, after rising above the horizon, makes short stops, and then goes faster until it reaches the noon point. So the Unknown inquired of them what was the matter with the sun. They denied having any knowledge about it, and said, "Somebody has to go there to see and examine." "Who would go there, and what could he do after he gets there?" The people said, "We are afraid to go up there." But the Unknown selected two men to make the ascent, gave to each a club, and instructed them that as soon as the wizard who was playing these tricks on the sun was leaving his cavern in the earth and appeared on the surface they should kill him on the spot. "It is a wizard who causes the sun to go so fast in the morning, for at sunrise he makes dashes at it, and the sun, being afraid of him, tries to flee from his presence." The two brave men went to the rising place of the sun to watch the orifice from which the sun emerges. The wizard appeared at the mouth of the cave, and at the same time the sun was to rise from another orifice beyond it. The wizard watched for the fiery disk and put himself in position to rush and jump at it at the moment of its appearance. When the wizard held up his head the two men knocked it off from his body with their clubs, took it to their tribe, and proclaimed that they

---

[1] From A. S. Gatschet, Some Mythic Stories of the Yuchi Indians, American Anthropologist, Vol. VI, p. 281.

had killed the sorcerer who had for so long a time urged the sun to a quicker motion. But the wizard's head was not dead yet. It was stirring and moving about, and to stop this the man of mysterious origin advised the people to tie the head on the uppermost limbs of a tree. They did so, and on the next morning the head fell to the ground, for it was not dead yet. He then ordered them to tie the head to another tree. It still lived and fell to the ground the next day. To insure success, the Unknown then made them tie it to a red cedar tree. There it remained, and its life became extinct. The blood of the head ran through the cedar. Henceforth the grain of the wood assumed a reddish color, and the cedar tree became a medicine tree.[1]

14. The Origin of the White People and Their First Appearance to the Yuchi.

It was out upon the ocean. Some sea-foam formed against a big log floating there. Then a person emerged from the sea-foam and crawled out upon the log. He was seen sitting there. Another person crawled up, on the other side of the log. It was a woman. They were whites. Soon the Indians saw them, and at first thought that they were sea-gulls, and they said among themselves, "Are not they white people?" Then they made a boat and went out to look at the strangers more closely.

Later on the whites were seen in their house-boat. Then they disappeared.

In about a year they returned, and there were a great many of them. The Indians talked to them but they could not understand each other. Then the whites left.

But they came back in another year with a great many ships. They approached the Indians and asked if they could come ashore. They said, "Yes." So the whites landed, but they seemed to be afraid to walk much on the water. They went away again over the sea.

This time they were gone a shorter time; only three months passed and they came again. They had a box with them and asked the Indians for some earth to fill it. It was given to them as they desired. The first time they asked they had a square box, and when that was filled they brought a big shallow box. They filled this one too. Earth was put in them and when they were carried aboard the ship the white men planted seed in them and many things were raised. After they had taken away the shallow box, the whites came back and told the Indians that their land was very strong and fertile. So they asked the Indians to give them a portion of it that they might live on it. The Indians agreed to do it, the whites came to the shore, and they have lived there ever since.

---

[1] Cedar wood is always used in the manufacture of the flageolet (see Music) and cedar leaves are important agents in the medicinal practice (*q. v.*).

15. The Wolves Kill the Terrapin and Give the Terrapin Red Eyes.

The Terrapin was lying in a hollow. A Wolf came near and stood on the slope above the Terrapin. The Terrapin soon began to revile the Wolf, calling him bad names. Now the Wolf became very angry and straightway called his friends to help him punish the Terrapin. They gave chase and the Terrapin was compelled to crawl into a hollow log. They soon managed to get her out of this, but she got away and climbed up a grapevine into a tree. The wolves searched for her and at last saw her shadow. But they did not see where the Terrapin was, until afterwards. Then they began shooting at her and finally killed her with the old arrows which they picked up. The Wolf who was at the head of them told them what to do. So they tore her up. Then he took her head and held it up and asked who would eat it. The one whom he asked would not eat it. He said, "No! I will not eat it; it would give me a headache and kill me." He offered it to another one, and received the same answer. Each time he offered it to a wolf it was refused, and he could get no one to eat the Terrapin's head. Then the Wolf became very angry and took some of the blood and threw it in the eyes of the young terrapins who were standing around. That is why all terrapins have red eyes.

16. The Heron Outwits the Parrot.

The Parrot and the Heron were friends. They met one day and the Parrot asked the Heron to come over and visit him. The Heron was willing, so one day he went over to pay his visit. The Parrot was going to have dinner for him. When the food was ready, the Parrot put a flat dish full of it before the Heron and told him to eat away. But the dish was so flat that he could not get any of the food into his mouth. After trying a number of times he gave it up and decided to go home hungry. But before he left he asked the Parrot to come over and have dinner with him soon. Then he left.

Before long the Parrot went to dine with the Heron. The Heron had things ready and when they thought it time to eat, he got out his dinner. But now his dinner was in a high deep pot. This was all right for the Heron, but the Parrot could not get his bill near the food, because the pot was too deep. So he had to go home hungry himself, just as the Heron had to when he visited him. He was disappointed.

17. Rabbit Outwits Wolf and Steals Pigs.

The Rabbit and the Wolf were friends. One day the Rabbit said to the Wolf, "There are some fine pigs in a certain pen. I always kill and eat some. Let us go and get some now." So the Wolf agreed and they went to the place where some one had some fine hogs. "Now," said Rabbit to the Wolf, "you are the largest. You jump over the fence and knock one on the head and kill him. Throw him over the fence. You are the larger. You carry him and go on home and I will watch." The Wolf jumped over and got a good hog. He dragged him over the fence and started to carry him home. But the Rabbit had gone and cut a big pole. When the Wolf came along, Rabbit ran around his head and hit him with the pole. Then the Wolf dropped the hog and made off for home as fast as he could. He was struck hard, for he never looked back to see what it was. Now the Rabbit took the hog and carried it home with him. All night he roasted meat and had a good time.

Then he thought, "I have hit my good friend, I must go and see him." He laughed a great deal. Then he went to the Wolf's house to see him. "What was the matter with you?" he asked him. "They whipped me," said the Wolf. "Yes, I heard you making a din and I ran off," said Rabbit.

18.   RABBIT AND WOLF GO COURTING.

The Rabbit and the Wolf were fond of two girls. But the girls would often make fun of the Rabbit because he was smaller and weaker than the Wolf. "Well, I am smarter than Wolf, and you will see," said he at last.

Soon he met the Wolf, who was on his way to the girls' house. The Wolf wanted company so he asked Rabbit to go with him. "No," said Rabbit, "I am too tired." "Well, never mind, get up on my back and ride," the Wolf told him. Then the Rabbit agreed, and mounted the Wolf's back. "But you must go slowly. I am sore," he said. Soon they arrive at the house. "Now, I'll go and knock on the door, you wait here," said the Rabbit. Then he knocks on the door, and when the girls come, he says to them, "See the Wolf hitched out there. He is my horse. I'll drive him in." Then he goes out and tells the Wolf that the girls are ready and want to see them. He mounts the Wolf's back again. Then he digs his spurs into the Wolf and whips him up. They dash through the door, and almost break down the house. "See! I told you so," shouted the Rabbit as he rushed by the frightened girls.

19.   THE RABBIT IS TRAPPED BY THE TAR-MAN, AND ESCAPES.

Now the Rabbit used to steal beans from a certain man. He would go to the place where the beans were kept, during the night, and steal as many as he needed. The man made up his mind to catch the Rabbit. So he got some tar (*yasocĭ'*, 'pine drops,') and made a little man out of it. He put a stick in its hand and laid it near where the beans were the next night. Again the Rabbit went to steal beans. But when he got to the place and saw the tar-man there with a stick, he became angry, and told the little man that if he did not drop the stick, he would kick him. Then he kicked him, but his foot stuck to the tar-man, and Rabbit then told him that, unless he let go, he would kick him again. So he kicked him again, and that foot, too, got stuck. Then Rabbit told him that, if he did not let go now, he would hit him.   Then he hit the little man and his hand stuck where he hit the tar.   Rabbit then told him the same thing as before, and when he hit him with the other hand that stuck too.   So the Rabbit was well trapped.

In the morning the owner of the beans came to see what had happened. He laughed when he saw Rabbit caught there, and got everything ready to loosen the Rabbit and put him in a box.   But Rabbit escaped from the man and ran away.   Then the man put the tar-man among the beans again.   Before many nights had passed Rabbit came again for beans, and the same thing happened as before.   Rabbit quarreled with the tar-man and soon was trapped hand and foot.   Now this time the owner of the beans came and when he found Rabbit caught again he made sure that he would not escape.   He got him safely in a box, and said, "To-morrow I'll throw you in the river."   He left Rabbit all night.   Now before the time came for the man to throw him into the river, Rabbit was determined to escape.

The man's son was playing around near the box where Rabbit was, and soon Rabbit said to him, "Let me out, and you get in here; they are going to throw me into the river."   So the boy did open the box and got in himself. Then the Rabbit ran away.   The man threw the boy into the river.   That was his son, but he did not know it.

20.   The Rabbit Visits the Bear and Fails to Imitate Him.

The Bear and the Rabbit were friends.   The Rabbit went to visit the Bear and to have dinner with him.   Before they were ready to eat, the Bear went upstairs and cut some fat from his entrails.   Then he cooked it with the beans.   The dinner was very good, and Rabbit thought about it and made up his mind to do the same as the Bear when he wanted to have a fine dinner. Then the Rabbit told the Bear to come to see him.   Said he, "I live in the raspberry patch.   You must come to dinner."

Soon the Bear went over to the Rabbit's house and visited him.   Before dinner the Rabbit went upstairs to cut some fat from his entrails.   But when he cut his entrails he was hurt, and the pain was so great that he made a great uproar.   The Bear ran upstairs to see what was the matter, and found that Rabbit had cut his entrails.   "Now," said the Bear, "I'll show you how to do that."   And he cut some fat from himself and cooked it with the beans that Rabbit had prepared.   Then they had their dinner.   The Bear thought about it and went home laughing.

21.   Wildcat Feigns Death and Deceives the Rabbit.

The Wildcat was lying in a shady place in the woods.   They thought he was asleep.   The Rabbit came that way and found him lying there.   So he called the Turkeys and told them that the Wildcat was dead and lying not far away.   They assembled and made ready for a good time.   A rattle was brought and they began to dance, round and round the Wildcat.   Then they thought they might as well eat him.   But suddenly the Wildcat jumped up among them.   He caught the Rabbit and a fat Turkey.

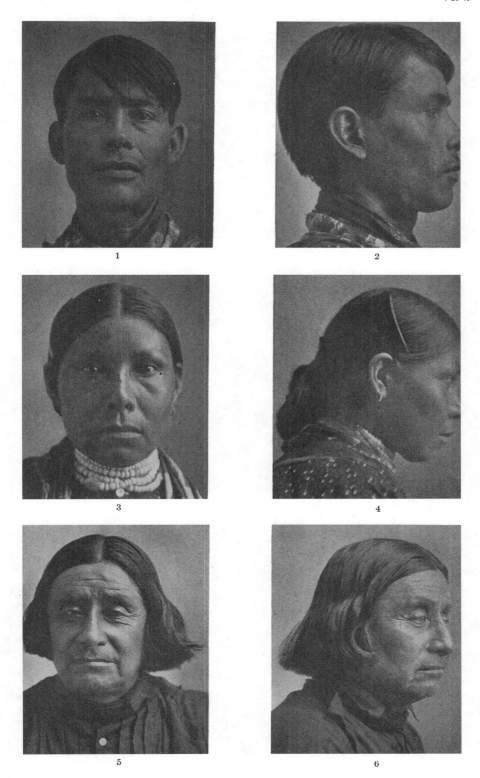

PORTRAITS OF YUCHI MEN AND WOMEN (FULL FACE AND PROFILE).

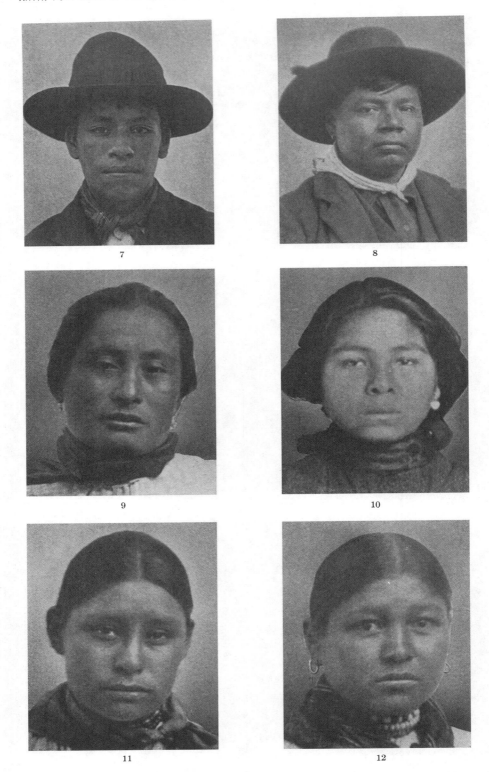

PORTRAITS OF YUCHI MEN AND WOMEN.

TYPES OF YUCHI POTTERY, MORTAR AND PESTLE.

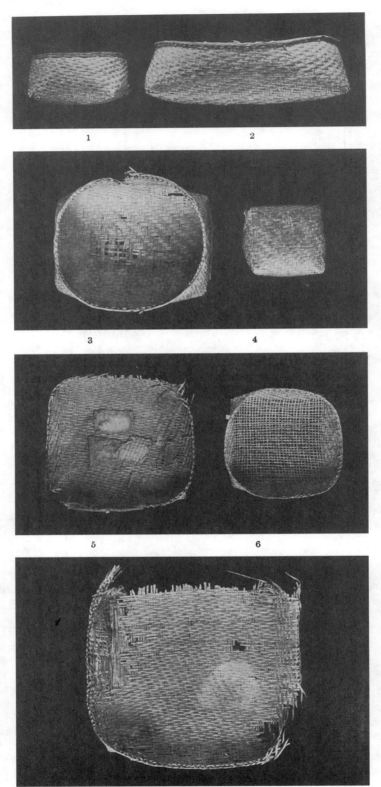

1

2

3

4

5

6

7

TYPES OF YUCHI BASKETRY.

BUCKSKIN COAT (CHEROKEE).

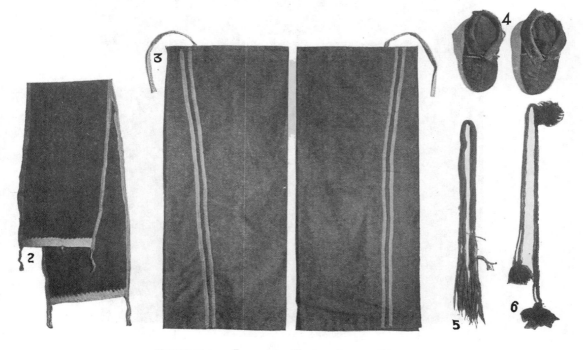

BREECHCLOTH, LEGGINGS, MOCCASINS AND SASHES.

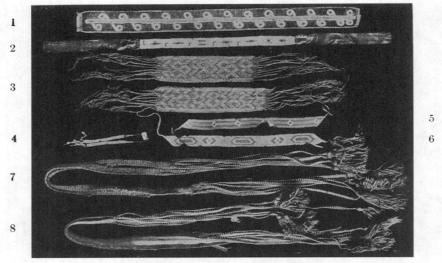

1
2
3
4
7
8
5
6

SASHES, GARTERS AND NECKBANDS

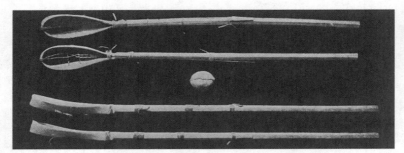

BALL STICKS AND BALL.

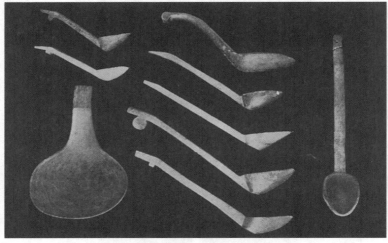

SPOONS AND LADLES.

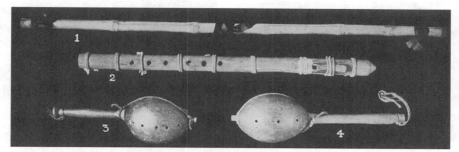

MEDICINE PIPE, FLAGEOLET AND RATTLES.

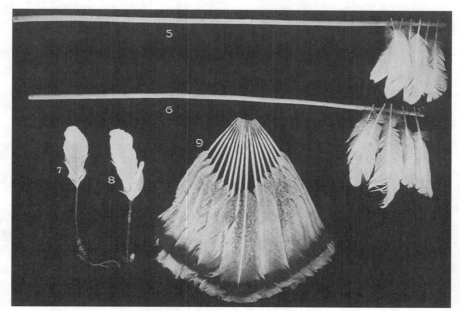

DANCE WANDS, FEATHER TREMBLERS AND FAN.

TORTOISE SHELL LEG RATTLES.

YUCHI BEADWORK DESIGNS.   (See page 56.)

YUCHI PICTURES, DRAWINGS AND DESIGNS. (See page 57.)

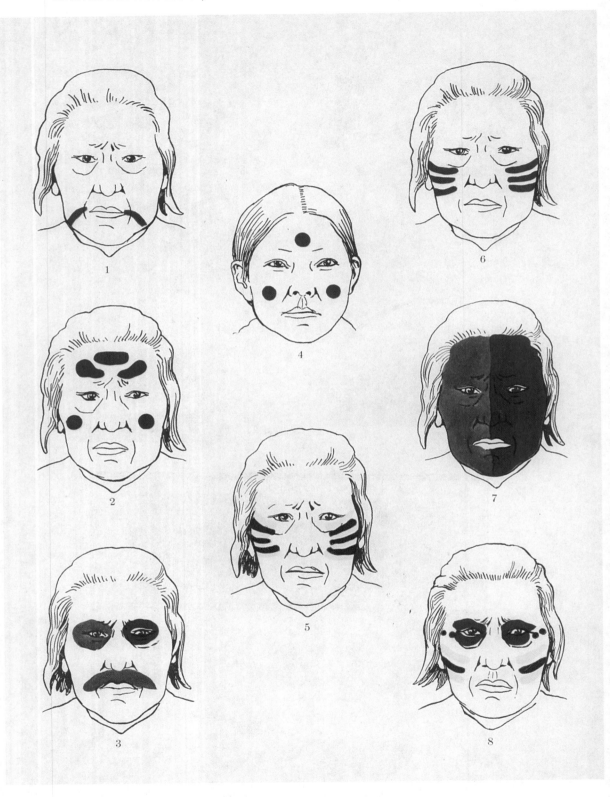

YUCHI FACIAL PAINTING.   (See page 76.)

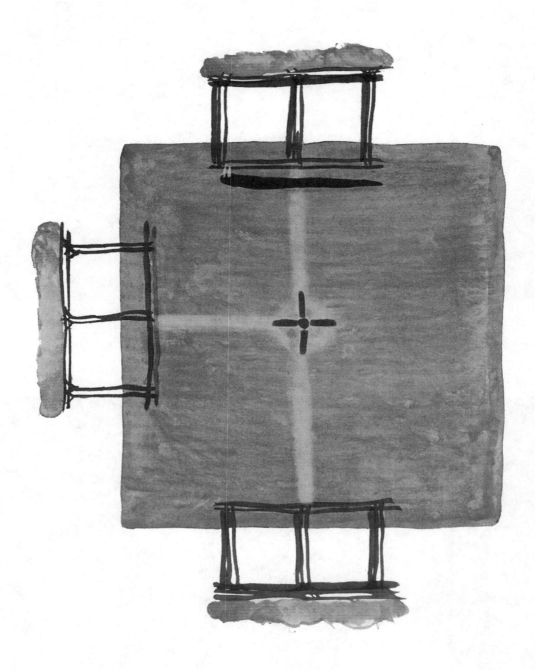

SYMBOLISM OF THE PUBLIC SQUARE-GROUND.   (See page 111.)

1. BIG TURTLE DANCE. FIRST NIGHT, ANNUAL CEREMONY.

2. BIG TURTLE DANCE. FIRST NIGHT, ANNUAL CEREMONY.

1.   NEW FIRE RITE.   SECOND DAY, ANNUAL CEREMONY.

2.   OFFICIALS PREPARING MEDICINE PLANTS.   SECOND DAY, ANNUAL CEREMONY.

1. The Scratching Operation. Second Day, Annual Ceremony.

2. The Scratching Operation Concluded. Second Day, Annual Ceremony.

1. The Rite of the Emetic. Second Day, Annual Ceremony.

2. The Rite of the Emetic Concluded. Second Day, Annual Ceremony.

1

2

3

SCENES AT THE BALL GAME. SECOND DAY, ANNUAL CEREMONY.

INDEX

Having been compiled by the introducer for the Nebraska paperback edition, this index reflects current knowledge of Yuchi ethnography and, more generally, the development of scholarship. Thus it reflects common English terms in use among the Yuchi (ca. 1993–2003) but not used by Speck. Examples of such terms include *poleboy*, *speaker*, *doctoring*, *Soup Dance*, and *grave houses*. Beyond their value for Yuchi readers, such terms will allow non-Yuchi readers to make connections between this work and other recently published sources. Similarly, the index includes terms such as *Orpheus*, *dual organization*, *Native American Church*, *body techniques*, and *Plains Sign Talk*, which were not known or widely used in 1909 but relate to contemporary discussions in anthropology and Native American studies. The modern scientific names of important plants have been added in similar fashion.